PROBLEM SOLVING
Step-By-Step
Teacher's Edition

Metropolitan Teaching and Learning Company
33 Irving Place
New York, New York 10003

Printed in the United States of America

ISBN: 1-58120-715-8

Problem Solving, Step-By-Step

Program Author: Jack Beers

Edited and Designed by Curriculum Concepts

Editor: Ralph Penner

Production Supervisor: Lucy Hebard

Designer: Kay Wanous

Cover Design: Jill Yutkovitch

Metropolitan Teaching and Learning Company
33 Irving Place
New York, New York 10003

Printed in the United States of America

ISBN: 1-58120-715-8

10 9 8 7 6 5 4 3 2

INTRODUCTION

This book is designed to help your students become better problem solvers and to score higher on the problem-solving portion of standardized tests. It is built on a teaching approach that uses a few powerful thinking strategies over and over. Repeated use of these strategies helps students to make them part of their permanent problem-solving tool kit and improve their test scores. These strategies are:

- **Decide What to Do First**
  For problems that have more than one step or where a misstep is common, students are given real help in deciding what the first step is.
- **Find Needed Information**
  Students learn how to find information in graphic displays such as tables, graphs, diagrams, and complex word problems.
- **Show Information Another Way**
  For many problems, it is useful to show the information in another format such as a diagram, table, drawing, word sentence, word equation, or algebraic equation. Both visual and algebraic tools are stressed.
- **Decide on the Kind of Answer You Need**
  Students learn to decide what form the answer should take: whether or not it is a number, what kind of unit it has, and whether an estimate will suffice.

LESSON STRUCTURE

Each lesson has four parts that move students from initial instruction to test preparedness.

- **Instruction** includes several examples and is interactive.
- **Guided Practice** focuses on process skills and each step of the solution process.
- **Practice** provides several problems to be solved from start to finish.
- **Test-Taking Practice** provides multiple choice items and writing tasks to prepare students for all items that they will see on standardized tests.

HOW TO USE THIS BOOK

The sequence of chapters in this book closely parallels the sequence of topics in a mathematics textbook for Grade 5. Each problem-solving lesson contains math content that is normally taught in that chapter. For example, the lesson on Explaining the Problem in your own Words in Chapter 8 requires some familiarity with variables and expressions. This is indicated in the running foot at the bottom of each page in the lesson.

Here are two ways of using the book that the author recommends:

1. **Use about one lesson per week in the sequence that they are listed in the book.** The Table of Contents will help you match up the math content with your textbook.
2. **For more intensive work on particular problem-solving topics, such as bar graphs, have students work on topical lessons in order.** The list of topics on page vi will help you find the lessons you need.

STEP 5 • Table of Contents

STEP 5 • *Topics*

Tables
1.3 Reading Tables
5.1 Using a Table to Rename Measures
9.2 Making a Rate Table

Bar Graphs
1.2 Reading Bar Graphs
4.6 Reading a Double-Bar Graph

Line Graphs
4.2 Reading a Line Graph
4.3 Interpreting Changes in a Line Graph

Circle Graphs
4.5 Reading a Circle Graph

Multi-Step Problems
2.4 Writing a Word Equation
3.5 Solving Multi-Step Problems
10.2 Deciding How to Estimate
10.3 Writing a Word Equation
10.4 Writing Word Equations

Estimation/Number Sense
1.1 Eliminating Wrong Answer Choices
2.1 Estimate or Exact Answer?
2.2 What Is the Question?
6.1 Using Benchmarks
7.2 Is the Computed Number the Answer?
10.4 Writing Word Equations

Representing Problems Differently
3.1 Using Simpler Numbers
3.6 Writing an Equivalent Problem
5.2 Deciding How to Rename Customary Measures
5.3 Deciding How to Show Measures Another Way
7.1 Drawing a Picture to Rename Measures
7.3 Using Models
10.3 Writing a Word Equation

Proportional Thinking
9.1 Writing Equal Ratios
9.2 Making a Rate Table
9.3 What Are the Units?

Algebraic Thinking
2.4 Writing a Word Equation
7.1 Drawing a Picture to Rename Measures
8.1 Explaining the Problem in Your Own Words
8.2 Drawing a Number Line
10.3 Writing a Word Equation
11.1 Using Formulas

Visual Thinking
4.1 Organizing a List
7.3 Using Models
10.1 Drawing a Number-Line Segment
11.2 Drawing Examples
12.1 Making a Table to Show Possible Outcomes
12.2 Making a Tree Diagram

Answer Interpretation
2.1 Estimate or Exact Answer?
2.2 What Is the Question?
3.3 Interpreting the Quotient
3.4 Which Answer Makes Sense?
7.2 Is the Computed Number the Answer?
9.3 What Are the Units?

Recognizing Important Information
2.3 Underlining Information
3.2 Underlining Information
4.4 Finding Data in a News Article
6.2 Drawing a Number Line

ASSESSMENT

Each lesson contains both multiple-choice items and writing items that can be used to assess students' progress in problem solving. In addition, these assessments will help prepare students for the style and content of items found on current state and standardized tests.

The multiple choice items include questions that ask about the process used to solve a problem -- without asking for the answer. Many states currently require that students can exhibit understanding in this way.

The WRITE ABOUT IT item or items that appear in each test are also similar to those on many state and standardized tests. Students need help developing the skills to do well on the writing assessments. The TEST-TAKING SKILL lessons that appear after chapters 2, 6, and 10 provide instruction and practice for writing assessments. They will help students learn to describe their plans and methods for solving problems. You can use these lessons at any time in the course of this book.

TEST-TAKING SKILLS

There are also additional TEST-TAKING SKILLS lessons at the end of chapters 4, 8, and 12. These skills relate to multiple-choice items. They can be used at any time.

TEACHING SUGGESTIONS

Chapter 1

Lesson 1

In this lesson, students analyze information in tables and then **Decide What to Do First**, which is to eliminate inappropriate answer choices.
Instruction: After students identify the title of the table, ask them to explain what they know about the table. Ask them to explain why Mars, 35,000,000, and 248,000,000 are in the same row.
Practice: Make sure that students understand that as the magnitude of a star becomes greater, the number representing the magnitude becomes smaller.

Lesson 2

In this lesson, students **Find Needed Information** in bar graphs and use it to solve problems.
Instruction: Ask students to explain what they know about the bar graph. They should understand the relationship between the vertical axis and the horizontal axis. Have students explain in their own words what the break in the bar graph means.
Test-Taking Practice: Allow students an opportunity to explain what the intervals are in the bar graph.

Lesson 3
In this lesson, students **Find Needed Information** in tables, and use it to solve problems.
Instruction: Discuss with students the fact that the numbers in the Area column represent millions of square miles.
Practice: It is important for students to understand that, in this table, areas are listed in actual millions of square miles. You may want to have students compare this table to the table on page 13.

Chapter 2
Lesson 1
In this lesson, students **Decide on the Kind of Answer Needed** to determine whether they need an exact answer or can estimate.
Instruction: Guide students to see that when a problem asks whether a computed value will be greater than or less than a certain threshold, an estimate may be sufficient to answer the question.
Test-Taking Practice: Make sure students distinguish accurately between situations in which an estimate is sufficient and situations in which an exact answer is required.

Lesson 2
In this lesson, students explain a problem in their own words to help them **Decide on the Kind of Answer Needed**.
Guided Practice: For problem 1, students may see that the question can be answered without actually computing the sum.
Test-Taking Practice: For problem 4, make sure students understand that they need to find the number of green triangles necessary for the pattern.

Lesson 3
In this lesson, students underline to **Find Needed Information** in a problem that has unnecessary information.
Instruction: Guide students to see that, by isolating the information they need to answer a question, they can solve a problem more quickly and easily.
Guided Practice: Make sure students understand that, although Versions A and B of the problem contain the same words, they will need to use different information to solve problems 1 and 2.
Practice: Particularly for problem 6, make sure students understand that all information can be found in the problem, such as the number of minutes for which Tim reads.

Lesson 4
In this lesson, students write a multi-step word problem in their own words to help them **Decide What to Do First**.
Instruction: Sometimes, students may think that they can solve any problem with a few simple arithmetic calculations.
Students will find it helpful to learn to use algebra as a tool. By

rewriting a problem as a word equation, students can focus on what they know and what they don't know. Encourage students to see that each word or phrase stands for a number. Then they can use the numbers they have to find the numbers they don't have.

Test-Taking Practice: Make sure students understand how to set up and interpret a word equation correctly.

Chapter 3

Lesson 1

In this lesson, students **Decide What to Do First** by substituting simpler numbers in a problem.
Instruction: Guide students to see that by substituting simpler numbers they can decide which operation to use. This way, students can more easily focus on how to plan to solve a problem. Solving the problem with simpler numbers also provides a handy approximate check for the actual computation.
Test-Taking Practice: For problem 5, students should show the solution with simpler numbers first. Then they should show the actual computation to find the exact answer. Ask students to generalize about the use of simpler numbers.

Lesson 2

In this lesson, students underline relevant data to **Find Needed Information.**
Instruction: Ask students to explain why they did not underline certain information.

Lesson 3

In this lesson, students interpret the quotient in division problems to **Decide on the Kind of Answer Needed**.
Instruction: Students who might have difficulty interpreting remainders should benefit from these clear illustrations of three situations that make use of the same numbers.
Guided Practice: Direct students' attention to the problem-solving tips near the top of the page.

Lesson 4

In this lesson, students **Decide on the Kind of Answer Needed** and underline the relevant information.
Instruction: Point out to students that when multiplication and division problems involve decimals, answers may need to be rounded to make sense.
Practice: For problem 4, remind students that money amounts need to be rounded to the nearest cent. Allow students an opportunity to compare problems 3 and 4 and draw a general conclusion about when money amounts need to be exact or may be rounded.

Lesson 5

In this lesson, students **Decide What to Do First** when confronted with a great deal of information in a multi-step problem.

Instruction: Remind students that multi-step problems often require that some steps be performed in a particular order. Writing word equations is a good way to organize information and helps you decide what to do first.

Test-Taking Practice: For problem 5, students should show that they know they must first find the total cost of the rentals. Then they can subtract to find the correct change.

Lesson 6

In this lesson, students write equivalent problems to **Show Information Another Way.**

Instruction: Remind students that any multiplication problem can be rewritten as an equivalent division problem. The reverse is true, as well.

Chapter 4

Lesson 1

In this lesson, students organize lists to **Show Information Another Way** when they are presented with a large amount of data.

Instruction: Point out to students that they can organize information in more than one way.

Guided Practice: Make sure students are aware that negative temperatures are degrees below zero and that the greater the number, the lower the temperature.

Lesson 2

In this lesson, students **Find Needed Information** by reading a line graph.

Instruction: Students should correctly identify the intervals in the graph. To do this, they should understand that the range of the graph is 10 degrees.

Guided Practice: Call students' attention to the boxed note on the page, and remind them that the break in the graph means that no pertinent information exists between 0°F and 30°F.

Lesson 3

In this lesson, students **Find Needed Information** to solve problems by interpreting changes in a line graph.

Instruction: Emphasize the importance of the steepness and direction of the slopes of the lines in line graphs.

Guided Practice: Make sure students understand that, for two time periods to have the same increase or decrease in value, the two lines must have the same steepness of slope.

Lesson 4

In this lesson, students **Find Needed Information** by

underlining relevant information in a news article.
Guided Practice: Make sure students realize that the sales totals for August and September are the same.

Lesson 5
In this lesson, students interpret a circle graph to **Find Needed Information** to solve problems.
Instruction: Point out to students that a 90° central angle in a sector of a circle graph indicates a sector that is one-quarter of the whole. Students can use this fact as a benchmark for estimation.
Test-Taking Practice: For problem 6, if students need help, remind them of the one-quarter benchmark to help them see that every group in the graph has at least 10 cards.

Lesson 6
In this lesson, students compare the bars of a double-bar graph to **Find Needed Information** to solve problems.
Instruction: Point out to students that a double-bar graph is much like a bar graph. A double-bar graph simply presents two pieces of like information side by side.

Chapter 5
Lesson 1
In this lesson, students use a table of measures to **Show Information Another Way**. This helps them to compare quantities given in different measures.
Instruction: To be sure that students don't lose sight of the final answer they are looking for, suggest that they write the problem in sentence form with a question mark: 2 kg ? 200 g. Then, having found 2 kg in grams, they can substitute: 2,000 g > 200 g. Point out that multiplying to find the larger unit in terms of a smaller unit is often easier than dividing.
Guided Practice, Practice: Encourage students having trouble distinguishing the values of the metric units to spell them out (for example, milliliter for mL) to avoid confusion.
Test-Taking Practice: Students need to understand that they are being asked not to find the answers to problems 1 - 3 but to choose a correct step in the process of finding the answers.

Lesson 2
In this lesson, students **Find Needed Information** by renaming customary units of measure.
Instruction: Ask students to explain why it is a good idea in the example to rename the measurement that is given in mixed units. (Multiplying and then adding to find total feet is probably easier than dividing and then interpreting the remainder as other units.)

This problem may also be solved by estimation. Have a volunteer show how: 11 yd 2 ft is greater than 11 yd, or 33 ft;

so, 11 yd 2 ft is also greater than 32 ft. This method might also be used to verify the calculated answer.
Guided Practice: Point out how the answer to the second example on this page could be checked by using the opposite operation from the one used to solve. (36 qt divided by 4 qt/gal = 9 gallons)
Practice: For problem 7, students should understand that the term "better buy" has a specific meaning–a greater quantity of a product at the same price. Other issues, such as quality, are not considered.

Lesson 3
In this lesson, students represent customary measures in drawings to decide on the operation and to **Decide on the Kind of Answer Needed**.
Instruction: Many students will rename feet and inches, as well as some other customary units, on a decimal basis, either carelessly or from lack of understanding the customary interrelationships. Caution the students to keep in mind that there are 12 inches per foot unit, not 10, and to calculate accordingly.
Test-Taking Practice: Students should understand that writing customary units in simplest form is sometimes a necessary step in finding the answer. In problem 5, the calculated sum, 112 lb 17 oz, needs to be simplified to 113 lb 1 oz to find the right answer choice.

Chapter 6
Lesson 1
In this lesson, students are shown how to use fractional benchmarks to **Find Needed Information** that they use for comparing.
Instruction: Visual learners may better understand why a given fraction is closer to 0, to $\frac{1}{2}$, or to 1, by at first constructing number lines to accompany their mental estimation. For example, have students draw a number line from 0 to 1 marked off in $\frac{1}{16}$s. Then have them draw circles or dots at three of the points denominated in $\frac{1}{16}$s: one near 0, one near the middle of the number line, and one near 1. They should write fractions for their three points and then use the procedure for finding a nearby benchmark to verify what is shown on the number line for each.
Practice: Point out that in problem 7, two fractions- $2\frac{1}{8}$in. and $1\frac{7}{8}$in.- are equally close to 2 in. Ask how the correct answer can be determined then.

Lesson 2
In this lesson, students **Find Needed Information** to solve fraction problems by drawing and using a number line.
Instruction: In the previous lesson, students estimated to

compare fractions by deciding whether the fractions were close to 0, to $\frac{1}{2}$, or to 1. In this lesson they use the same three benchmarks to add and subtract fractions. Note that here, the benchmarks are used to approximate the position of fractions on a number line and then to visually estimate the answer if an exact answer is not needed.
Guided Practice: Students must understand that when they need an exact answer, they should not use benchmarks, unless they choose to check the answer for reasonableness.
Test-Taking Practice: The Write About It problem gives students an opportunity to generalize from their experience with specific fraction problems to formulating a procedure for estimating with fractions on a number line.

Chapter 7

Lesson 1

In this lesson, students **Show Information Another Way** by drawing pictures to rename measures.
Instruction: Suggest to students that they check their answers, especially when a problem involves both calculating with fractions and renaming measures. Have a volunteer demonstrate how to check the answer to the example: Does 20 pt equal $2\frac{1}{2}$ gal? (20 pt ÷ 2 pt per qt = 10 qt; 10 qt ÷ 4 qt per gal = $2\frac{1}{2}$ gal; so, yes, the answer checks.)

Lesson 2

This lesson guides students to **Decide on the Kind of Answer Needed** .
Instruction: In Example 1, some students may question whether $3\frac{1}{3}$ batches of muffins is a sensible answer. Point out that the extra flour that $\frac{1}{3}$ of a batch stands for could go to make one or more extra muffins or to make bigger muffins than the recipe called for. In Example 2, by contrast, $\frac{3}{8}$ boat does not make sense as an answer, because a fraction of a boat cannot be used.

Lesson 3

In this lesson, students **Show Information Another Way** by using pictorial models to divide fractions.
Instruction: The model used in this lesson may easily be extended to examples involving mixed-number dividends. In Example 2, if Mr. Woo had $4\frac{2}{3}$ ft of foil, the model would be modified to show $4\frac{2}{3}$ boxes. The division by $\frac{2}{3}$ would then proceed as before.
Guided Practice: Students must understand that it is the dividend—the quantity to be divided—that should be represented in drawing the model. The divisor is the part or group of parts that students mark off in the model, a certain number of times, to determine the answer.

Chapter 8

Lesson 1

In this lesson, students **Show Information Another Way** by explaining problems in their own words.
Instruction and Practice: Guide students to see that writing a problem in their own words as a word equation can lead them quickly to writing a mathematical equation. By identifying the number they don't know, they know where to use a variable and generate an algebraic equation.
Test-Taking Practice: For item 7, make sure students understand that they must first subtract $3 from $5.50 before dividing to find the cost of one pen.

Lesson 2

In this lesson, students use number lines to **Find Needed Information** to add and subtract integers.
Instruction: If students seem uncomfortable working with negative integers, remind them that addition and subtraction still function basically the same way they do in those operations with positive integers.

Chapter 9

Lesson 1

In this lesson, students **Show Information Another Way** as a number sentence made up of two equal ratios.
Instruction: Students might find it helpful to think of writing equal ratios as similar to writing equivalent fractions.

Lesson 2

In this lesson, students **Show Information Another Way**, making rate tables to show the information they need to solve problems.
Instruction: Make sure students understand that, to make a rate table, they can add the original value to itself again and again.
Test-Taking Practice: Check to make sure that students correctly complete the rate table.

Lesson 3

In this lesson, students use proportions to help to **Decide on the Kind** of Answer Needed, which is often a unit rate.
Instruction: Make sure students set up their proportions correctly.

Chapter 10

Lesson 1

In this lesson, students draw number-line segments to **Show Information Another Way**.
Instruction: Make sure students recognize the use of 25%, 50%, and 75% as benchmarks for their estimation process.
Guided Practice: For problem 1, make sure that students recognize 33% and 67% as benchmarks that approximate one-

third and two-thirds.
Test-Taking Practice: For the Write About It, point out to students that they are putting together a general idea about how to use number-line segments to estimate percents. Ask students to think of other cases in which they could use number-line segments for estimation.

Lesson 2

In this lesson, students use benchmarks as they **Decide What to Do First** to estimate percents and determine whether to calculate an exact answer.
Instruction: Remind students that the decision to estimate first tells them not only whether they need an exact answer or not but also provides a handy check for reasonableness if they must calculate an exact answer.

Lesson 3

In this lesson, students **Show Information Another Way** by rewriting a problem as a word equation to solve percent problems.
Instruction: Encourage students to see that reducing a word problem to a word equation can make clear the question that the problem poses.
Test-Taking Practice: For the Write About It, encourage students to recognize other situations in which writing an equation can direct them toward solving a problem.

Lesson 4

In this lesson, students can **Decide on the Kind of Answer Needed** for problems that have more than two steps by writing word equations.
Instruction: Lead students to recognize that they can solve multi-step problems more easily if they identify the questions they need to answer and write word equations to represent those questions. These equations will help students identify the kind of answer they need.
Guided Practice and Practice: Encourage students to use benchmarks to estimate the percents that sectors of a circle graph represent.

Chapter 11

Lesson 1

In this lesson, students learn to **Show Information Another Way** by using formulas.
Instruction: Explain that the parentheses call for computation inside the parentheses first. For Example 1, this means adding 20 + 12 before multiplying by 2. Also, discuss how each of the perimeter formulas shows the perimeter. First, choose specific numbers such as 6 and 5 for the sides of the parallelogram. Show how the sum is written 6 + 5 + 6 + 5, or as 2 x (6 + 5). Next, discuss how the problem is done for all other parallelograms.

Guided Practice and Practice: In the table of formulas, and in problem 2 of the Guided Practice, an exponent is used to show the formula for area of a square. Explain that the raised 2, or exponent, means that the value of s, the side length, is used as a factor two times. Students may also think of the formula as A = s x s, or as "Area equals side times side." Remind students that area is always in square units.

Lesson 2

Students learn to **Show Information Another Way** by drawing geometric figures.

Instruction: Be sure that students understand the logic of the example: The statement must be either true or false. If just one figure can be created that contradicts the statement, then the statement is false; no further work need be done. If no figure exists that contradicts the statement, then it is true. But caution students to think hard about all possibilities that might prove the statement false.

Guided Practice: Explain that these examples have a different logic. There are three possible results to the students' investigations. However, the use of examples to support or contradict the statements is the same.

Practice: It is a good idea to give students plenty of time to explore the possibilities of figures, because it is easy to overlook a contradictory example and time-consuming to thoroughly consider supporting examples.

Test-Taking Practice: In the Write About It problem, students are challenged to demonstrate a conceptual understanding of the method of deriving solutions and asked to express this understanding in a specific way.

Chapter 12

Lesson 1

In this lesson, students **Find Needed Information** by making a table of possible outcomes.

Guided Practice : Point out how the ordered-pair format is important to distinguishing combinations. Have students decide whether (Blue, Black) and (Black, Blue) are different and why.

Practice: At the end of the lesson, have students generalize about the number of outcomes if there are 3 outcomes for the first event, 5 for the second. Then, ask students to generalize about a case in which there are m outcomes for the first and n for the second.

Lesson 2

In this lesson, students **Show Information Another Way** by making a tree diagram.

Instruction: Be sure students can read the tree diagram on page 171. Ask: If a result is tails, heads, tails, where does that show up on the tree diagram?

Guided Practice: Work through how the first four outcomes in problem 1 were determined. Have students write all the combinations for Spinner A and then branch to show all the possibilities for Spinner B.

PROBLEM SOLVING
Step-By-Step

Metropolitan Teaching and Learning Company
33 Irving Place
New York, New York 10003

Printed in the United States of America

STEP 5 • Table of Contents

STEP 5 • Topics

Tables

1.3 Reading Tables
5.1 Using a Table to Rename Measures
9.2 Making a Rate Table

Bar Graphs

1.2 Reading Bar Graphs
4.6 Reading a Double-Bar Graph

Line Graphs

4.2 Reading a Line Graph
4.3 Interpreting Changes in a Line Graph

Circle Graphs

4.5 Reading a Circle Graph

Multi-Step Problems

2.4 Writing a Word Equation
3.5 Solving Multi-Step Problems
10.2 Deciding How to Estimate
10.3 Writing a Word Equation
10.4 Writing Word Equations

Estimation/Number Sense

1.1 Eliminating Wrong Answer Choices
2.1 Estimate or Exact Answer?
2.2 What Is the Question?
6.1 Using Benchmarks
7.2 Is the Computed Number the Answer?
10.4 Writing Word Equations

Representing Problems Differently

3.1 Using Simpler Numbers
3.6 Writing an Equivalent Problem
5.2 Deciding How to Rename Customary Measures
5.3 Deciding How to Show Measures Another Way
7.1 Drawing a Picture to Rename Measures
7.3 Using Models
10.3 Writing a Word Equation

Proportional Thinking

9.1 Writing Equal Ratios
9.2 Making a Rate Table
9.3 What Are the Units?

Algebraic Thinking

2.4 Writing a Word Equation
7.1 Drawing a Picture to Rename Measures
8.1 Explaining the Problem in Your Own Words
8.2 Drawing a Number Line
10.3 Writing a Word Equation
11.1 Using Formulas

Visual Thinking

4.1 Organizing a List
7.3 Using Models
10.1 Drawing a Number-Line Segment
11.2 Drawing Examples
12.1 Making a Table to Show Possible Outcomes
12.2 Making a Tree Diagram

Answer Interpretation

2.1 Estimate or Exact Answer?
2.2 What Is the Question?
3.3 Interpreting the Quotient
3.4 Which Answer Makes Sense?
7.2 Is the Computed Number the Answer?
9.3 What Are the Units?

Recognizing Important Information

2.3 Underlining Information
3.2 Underlining Information
4.4 Finding Data in a News Article
6.2 Drawing a Number Line

Name ____________________

Eliminating Wrong Answer Choices

Deciding what to do first can help you solve a test problem more easily. One way to begin is to eliminate answer choices that are clearly wrong.

Example

A. Read the problem carefully. Then look at the information given in the table. The table shows the longest and shortest distances from Earth of several planets. What is the shortest distance between any of these planets and Earth?

Distances to Planets in Our Solar System		
Planet	**Shortest Distance from Earth**	**Longest Distance from Earth**
Mars	35,000,000 mi	248,000,000 mi
Venus	25,000,000 mi	161,000,000 mi
Saturn	745,000,000 mi	1,031,000,000 mi

A 35,000,000 mi
B 1,031,000,000 mi
C 25,000,000 mi
D 10,000 mi

B. Look at each answer choice. Compare the answer choices with the distances given in the table.

- Choice B appears in the table under the "Longest Distance" category, so this choice cannot be correct. Cross out choice B.
- Choice D does not appear in the table, so it cannot be correct. Cross out choice D.
- The two remaining choices are A and C. Both choices appear in the table under the heading "Shortest Distance." Circle these choices.

C. To solve the problem, you need to compare only two choices instead of four.

Compare: 25,000,000 < 35,000,000

So, the correct choice is C, 25,000,000 **miles.**

GUIDED PRACTICE

Use the table to answer the questions.

Distances to Planets in Our Solar System		
Planet	Shortest Distance from Earth	Longest Distance from Earth
Mars	35,000,000 mi	248,000,000 mi
Venus	25,000,000 mi	161,000,000 mi
Saturn	745,000,000 mi	1,031,000,000 mi

1. Which choice shows the planets in order from farthest to nearest when each planet is at its farthest from Earth?
   A Mars, Saturn, Venus
   B Mars, Venus, Pluto
   C Saturn, Mars, Venus
   D Venus, Mars, Saturn

   a. Which answer choice contains a planet that is not in the table? B
   Cross out this answer choice.

   b. Which answer choice shows the planets in order from nearest to farthest?

   D **Cross out this answer choice.**

   c. Compare the remaining choices: A and C. Which choice shows the planets in order from farthest to nearest? C

2. The greatest distance from Earth to the sun during Earth's revolution around the sun is 94.6 million miles. Which choice below shows this number in standard form?
   J 94 million, 6 hundred thousand
   K 94,600,000
   L 90,000,000 + 4,000,000 + 600,000
   M 9,460,000,000

   Cross out each answer choice that you find to be wrong.

   a. Which answer choices are not written in standard form? J, L

   b. Answers K and M are not crossed out. Is there a fast way to eliminate one of them? Explain.

   Eliminate M because it's a number in the billions.

   c. The correct answer to the problem is K.

Name ____

PRACTICE

Use the table below to answer problems 3–8. You may want to cross out answer choices that are clearly wrong to help you solve each problem.

Magnitudes of Some Stars

Star	Magnitude
Vega	0.04
Rigel	0.14
Procyon	0.37
Betelgeuse	0.41
Achernar	0.51

The brightness of a star is called its *magnitude*. The *lower* the magnitude, the *brighter* the star.

3. **What is the magnitude of the brightest star named in the table?** D

   A 0.51
   B 0.37
   C 0.16
   D 0.04

4. **What is the magnitude of the least-bright star named in the table?** K

   J 0.03
   K 0.51
   L 0.41
   M 0.14

5. **What is the difference in magnitude between Rigel and Procyon?** C

   A 0.0023
   B 0.023
   C 0.23
   D 2.3

6. **What is the difference in magnitude between Procyon and Betelgeuse?** K

   J 0.004
   K 0.04
   L 0.4
   M 4.0

7. **What is the difference in magnitude between the brightest and the least-bright star?** B

   A 0.02
   B 0.47
   C 2.06
   D 2.47

8. **What is the name of the brightest star in the table?** L

   J Capella
   K Achernar
   L Vega
   M Rigel

TEST-TAKING PRACTICE

Use the table below to solve problems 1–5. Fill in the box of your choice in the space at the bottom. You may want to cross out clearly wrong choices.

Distance of Planets from Sun

Planet	Distance from Sun
Earth	93,000,000 mi
Jupiter	484,000,000 mi
Mars	142,000,000 mi
Mercury	36,000,000 mi
Neptune	2,800,000,000 mi
Pluto	3,700,000,000 mi
Saturn	888,000,000 mi
Uranus	1,800,000,000 mi
Venus	67,000,000 mi

1. **Based on the information in the table above, which planet do you think has the closest average distance from Earth?** D
   - **A** Mars
   - **B** Neptune
   - **C** Pluto
   - **D** Venus

2. **About how many times as far from the sun is Pluto than Mercury?** M
   - **J** about 36 times as far
   - **K** about 10 times as far
   - **L** about 1,000,000 times as far
   - **M** about 100 times as far

3. **Which answer choice shows the distances of the four closest planets to the sun in order from greatest to least?** C
   - **A** 36,000,000; 67,000,000; 93,000,000; 142,000,000
   - **B** 484,000,000; 900,000,000; 2,800,000,000; 3,700,000,000
   - **C** 142,000,000; 93,000,000; 67,000,000; 36,000,000
   - **D** 142,000,000; 67,000,000; 93,000,000; 36,000,000

4. **Which planet is the middle planet?** L
   - **J** Earth
   - **K** Saturn
   - **L** Jupiter
   - **M** Not given

Write About It

5. **Look again at problem 3 above. Explain how you solved the problem.**

   Answers will vary. Explanations may include eliminating answer choices that are in the wrong order. Look for accurate interpretation of data in table.

1. A ☐ B ☐ C ☐ D ☒   3. A ☐ B ☐ C ☒ D ☐

2. J ☐ K ☐ L ☐ M ☒   4. J ☐ K ☐ L ☒ M ☐

Name ______________________ **Chapter 1** **L2**

Reading Bar Graphs

To solve a problem, you sometimes have to find the information you need by reading a bar graph. Begin by looking at what the different parts of the graph tell you.

The graph at the right shows the maximum speeds of four mammals. The vertical axis is labeled **Speed** and shows the speeds in kilometers per hour. The horizontal axis is labeled **Mammal**. It shows the name of the mammal for each data entry.

The speeds in this graph are not exact. They have been rounded.

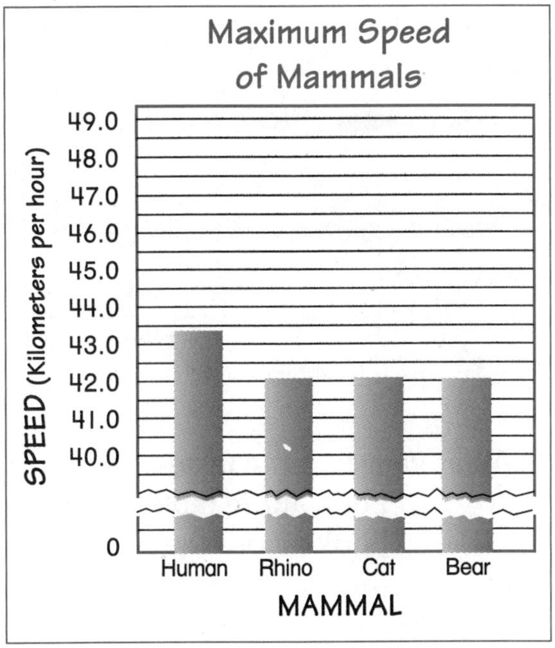

When a graph has a break, like this one, it means that all of the data is greater than the top edge of the break.

Example 1

What is the maximum speed of a human?

Step 1: Look for the bar that is labeled Human. The length of the bar shows you a human's maximum speed.

Step 2: Find the top of the bar. Move across the graph to the vertical axis.

The top of the bar is halfway between what two numbers?

__43.0__ **and** __44.0__

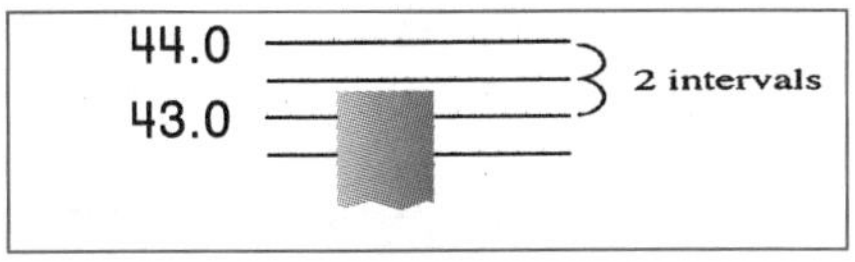

So, the maximum speed of a human is

__43.5__ **kilometers per hour.**

Notice the two intervals between 43.0 and 44.0. The line in between shows 43.5.

Example 2

Which mammal has a maximum speed of 45.0 kilometers per hour?

Step 1: Find the bar that stops at 45.0 kilometers per hour.

Step 2: Follow the bar to the horizontal axis.

Which name is below that bar? __Rhino__

So, the __Rhino__ **has a maximum speed of 45.0 kilometers per hour.**

GUIDED PRACTICE

Bar graphs can also be horizontal. Use the graph below to answer the questions.

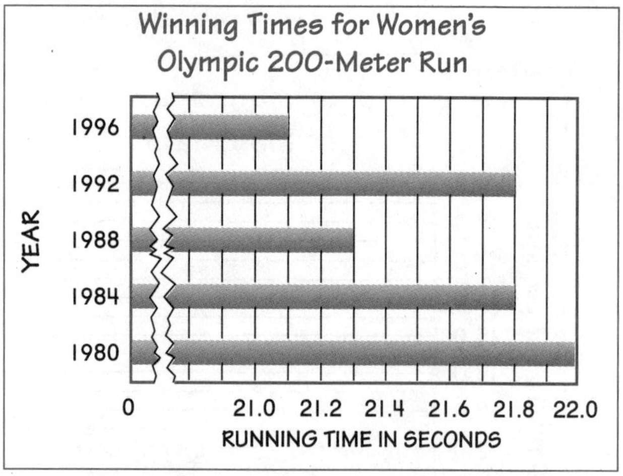

1. What year had the fastest winning time?
   Step 1: Look at the table. Find the shortest bar.
   Step 2: Look across the bar.

   What year is the bar for? 1996

   So, 1996 **was the year with the fastest winning time.**

2. At a track meet, the winning time for the women's 200-meter run is 0.4 second slower than the winning Olympic time in 1988.
   What is the winning time at the track meet?

   Step 1: Find the bar for 1988. **Where does the bar stop?** 21.3 seconds
   Step 2: Add.

   0.4 + 21.3 = 21.7 seconds

   So, the winning time at the track meet is 21.7 **seconds.**

3. **What is the combined time of all the winning times?**
   Step 1: Find the time that each bar shows.

   1980 22.0 s **1988** 21.3 s **1996** 21.1 s

   1984 21.8 s **1992** 21.8 s

   Step 2: Add the times for each year.

   22.0 + 21.8 + 21.3 + 21.8 + 21.1 = 108 s

   So, the combined time for all the years is 108 **seconds.**

Name ______________________________

Read the bar graph to find the information you need. You may mark or draw on the graph.

4. **What is the distance that Barry ran?** 5.2 **kilometers**

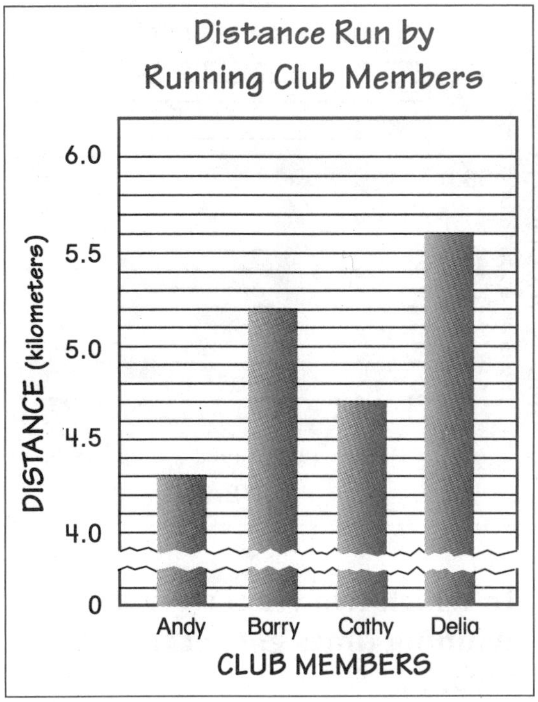

5. **Put the runners in order from the runner who ran the greatest distance to the runner who ran the least.**

   Delia, Barry, Cathy, Andy

6. **What does the break in the graph mean?**

   That all the club members shown in the graph ran at least 4.0 kilometers.

7. Tulin ran 1.3 kilometers farther than Delia ran.

   How far did Tulin run?

   6.9 kilometers

8. Cathy is training for a race. The race is 5 kilometers long. Before she runs in the race, she wants to be training at that distance.

   How much farther does Cathy need to run in order to train at the distance of the race?

   0.3 kilometers

9. The coach of the track club wants to know the total distance run by the four runners in the graph.

   What is the total distance that the four runners ran?

   19.8 kilometers

10. Last week Andy ran 2.2 kilometers less than the distance shown in the graph.

    How far did Andy run last week?

    2.1 kilometers

TEST-TAKING PRACTICE

Use the bar graph to solve the problems. Choose the best answer for each problem.

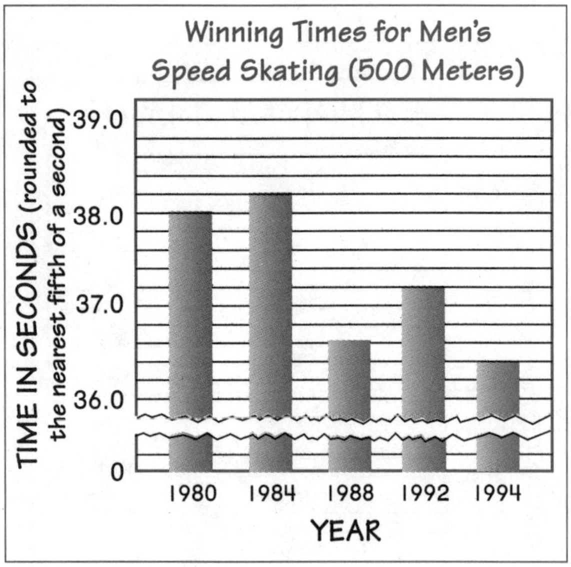

1. **In which two years were the winning times greater than 37.5 seconds?** A
   - **A** 1980 and 1984
   - **B** 1980 and 1992
   - **C** 1984 and 1992
   - **D** 1992 and 1994

2. At a regional meet, the winning time in the 500-meter event is 1.3 seconds slower than the time in 1988.

   What is the winning time at the regional meet? K
   - **J** 35.3 seconds
   - **K** 37.9 seconds
   - **L** 71.3 seconds
   - **M** 71.6 seconds

3. **What does the break in the graph mean?** B
   - **A** In every year, the winning skaters finished in under 36.0 seconds.
   - **B** In every year, the winning skaters finished in over 36.0 seconds.
   - **C** The skaters who did not win all finished in under 36.0 seconds.
   - **D** Not given

Write About It

Write a plan for solving the problem, and then solve it.

4. **What is the total combined time of all the winners from 1980 to 1994?**

   Find the winning times for each year:
   38.0 s, 38.2 s, 36.6 s, 37.2 s, 36.4 s.
   Then add; 38.0 + 38.2 + 36.6 +
   37.2 + 36.4 = 186.4 s. So, the total
   combined time for all the
   winners is 186.4 s.

1. A ☒ B ☐ C ☐ D ☐
2. J ☐ K ☒ L ☐ M ☐
3. A ☐ B ☒ C ☐ D ☐

Name ______________________________ Chapter 1 L3

Reading Tables

Sometimes, the information you need to solve a problem is in a table.

Land Area of World Regions

Region	Area (in millions of square miles)
Africa	11.7
North America	9.4
South America	6.9
Antarctica	5.4
Asia	17.4
Europe	3.8
Oceania (including Australia, New Zealand)	3.3

A. The title and labels of a table tell you what the table is about. **What is the table at the right about?**

Land areas of world regions in millions of square miles

B. The **data**, or pieces of information, in a table are given in columns and rows. The first column in this table is labeled "Region." **What data are in the "Region" column?**

The names of different regions of the world

What data are in the "Area" column?

The area of each region, given in millions of square miles

C. What is the land area of Africa?

Step 1: Find "Africa" in the first column.
Step 2: **Draw a line to the number *in the same row* of the second column.**
This number shows the land area of Africa in millions of square miles.

So, the land area of Africa is 11.7 **million square miles.**

D. Which region has the greatest land area?

Step 1: Compare the numbers in the second column.
Find the greatest number.
Step 2: **Draw a line to the name of the region in the same row.**
This is the region with the greatest land area.

So, the region with the greatest land area is Asia.

GUIDED PRACTICE

Complete the table, and answer the questions.

Gold Person Triathlon Results

Athlete	Swim	Bicycle	Run	Total Time
Frank	25 min	46 min	55 min	126 min
Janice	21 min	53 min	52 min	126 min
Leore	23 min	35 min	67 min	125 min

1. What is this table about?

   The times for three different athletes in the Gold Person Triathlon

2. Janice had the fastest time in the Swim. She finished in 21 minutes. **In the table, fill in Janice's swim time.**

   Step 1: Find Janice's name in the table.

   Step 2: Move your finger across the row to the **Swim** column. Fill in her time.

3. Who had the fastest time in the Run?

   Step 1: Find the **Run** column in the table.

   Step 2: Move your finger down the **Run** column, and find the shortest time.

   Step 3: Move your finger along the row with the shortest time to the name column.

   So, Janice had the fastest time in the Run.

4. Leore finished the Bicycle part of the race in 35 minutes.

   In the table, fill in her time.

Solve

Use the information in the table to solve each problem.

5. **Who had the fastest time in the Bicycle part of the race?**

   Leore

6. **Who had the slowest time in the Swim?**

   Frank

7. **What was Leore's time in the Run?**

   67 **minutes**

8. Who had the fastest time in all three parts of the race combined? **In the Total Time column fill in the total times for each person.**

   So, Leore had the fastest total time.

PRACTICE

Use the table to find the information you need to solve the problems. You may mark or draw lines on the table.

World Areas and Populations by Region

Region	Area (square miles)	Population 1994
North America	9,400,000	289,000,000
South America, Caribbean	6,900,000	474,000,000
Europe	3,900,000	509,000,000
Asia	17,200,000	3,344,000,000
Africa	11,700,000	701,000,000
Oceania (including Australia, New Zealand)	3,300,000	28,000,000
Antarctica	5,100,000	0

9. What is the table about?

The world areas and populations by region

10. What data does the third column give you?

The 1994 population of each region

11. What is the area of Oceania?

3,300,000 square miles

12. What was the population of Oceania in 1994?

28,000,000

13. Which region has an area of 5.1 million square miles?

Antarctica

14. Which region had a population of 509,000,000 in 1994?

Europe

15. Which region had the largest population in 1994?

Asia

16. Which region had the smallest population in 1994?

Antarctica

TEST-TAKING PRACTICE

Use the table to solve the problems. Choose the best answer for each problem. In the answer section at the bottom of this page, fill in the box of your choice.

Populations of Four of the World's Largest Cities

City	Population (millions in 1998)	Population (estimated millions in 2015)	Annual Growth Rate (percent)
Bombay	15.1	26.2	4.2
Mexico City	16.5	19.2	1.8
New York City	16.3	17.6	0.3
Tokyo	27.0	28.9	1.5

1. In the first two columns, what do the numbers show? B

A number of cities in the world
B number of people in a city
C number of people in the world
D number of people in a country

2. Which of the following sentences is false? M

J In the table, Tokyo is a city.
K The table has a column called "Annual Growth Rate."
L The table has a row called "New York City."
M Tokyo's population in 1998 was 26 million people.

3. Which city has an Annual Growth Rate of 0.3 percent? C

A Bombay **C** New York City
B Mexico City **D** Tokyo

Write About It

Write a plan for solving the problem, and then solve.

4. Which city has the least difference between its population in 1998 and its estimated population in 2015? How many more people will it have?

For each city, subtract the 1998 population from the estimated population for 2015.

Compare the numbers.

New York, 1.3 million more people.

1. A ❑ B ☒ C ❑ D ❑ 3. A ❑ B ❑ C ☒ D ❑

2. J ❑ K ❑ L ❑ M ☒

Name ______________________________

Estimate or Exact Answer?

Deciding on the kind of answer you need can often help you to solve a problem. Sometimes, you can estimate. At other times, you need an exact answer.

Example 1

Tony has $5. He wants to buy pretzels and a 2-liter bottle of soda for a party. Does he have enough money?

Snack Price List	
Pretzels	$1.89
Crackers	$1.99
Nuts	$2.19
2-liter soda	$1.59

Because the problem does not ask for a price or for a money amount, you do not need an exact answer. You can estimate to find out whether Tony has enough money.

Step 1: Estimate how much the two items will cost.

THINK: Round each number to the next-higher dollar.

$1.89 + **$1.59**

↓ ↓

$2 + $__2__ = $__4__

So, the two items cost about $ __4__.

Step 2: Because you rounded up, your estimate is higher than the exact sum would be. Compare the money Tony has to the estimated cost of the two items.

$5 > $4

Does Tony have enough money to buy both items? __yes__

Example 2

Janice has $11. Does she have enough money to buy one package of nuts each week for 4 weeks?

Step 1: Round the cost of a package of nuts to the nearest dollar.

Round $2.19 to $__2__.

Step 2: Multiply to find the total cost of 4 packages of nuts.

4 x $__2__ **= $**__8__

$__8__ **< $11**

Does Janice have enough money? __yes__

GUIDED PRACTICE

1. Alex had $10. He bought 20 stamps for $6 at the post office. How much money does he have left?

Does the problem require an exact answer, or can you estimate? Explain.

Exact answer. The question asks for an exact money amount.

Solve the problem. $ 10.00 **– $6 = $** 4

So, Alex has $ 4.00 **left after buying 20 stamps.**

2. Is the sum of 33, 87, and 48 greater than 200?
Does the problem require an exact answer, or can you estimate? Explain, then solve.

Estimate. If you round each number up, and the total is less than 200, you don't need to find the exact sum.

Step 1: Round each number up.

Round 33 up to 40.

Round 87 up to 90.

Round 48 up to 50.

Step 2: Add.

40 + 90 + 50 = 180

Step 3: Compare the sum to 200.

180 < 200

Is the sum of 33, 87, and 48 greater than 200? no

3. In 1998, the Science Museum had 155,398 visitors. In 1999, it had 182,045 visitors. About how many more people visited the museum in 1999 than in 1998?

Does the problem require an exact answer, or can you estimate? Explain.

Estimate. The question asks about how many.

Solve.

Step 1: Round both numbers to the nearest ten thousand.

Round 155,398 to 160,000.

Round 182,045 to 180,000.

Step 2: Subtract.

180,000 – 160,000 = 20,000

The museum had about 20,000 **more visitors in 1999 than in 1998.**

Name ____________________

PRACTICE

Decide whether you must give an exact answer or an estimate. Then solve.

4. Jennifer earns $9 per week. She wants to buy her mother a clock that costs $50. If she saves for 4 weeks, will she have enough money?

Estimate.

4 x 10 = 40

Will Jennifer have enough money?

no

5. An amusement park had 342,981 guests in June and 478,982 guests in July. About how many people visited the parks in the two months?

Estimate.

300,000 + 500,000 = 800,000

About 800,000 people visited the park in June and July.

6. Ed has $175 to spend on tires for his van. If each tire costs $37, how many tires can he buy?

Estimate.

180 ÷ 40 → 4 r20 → 4

Ed can buy 4 tires.

7. Tyrone works at a computer store. A customer buys $238 worth of software. He gives Tyrone $300. How much change should the customer receive?

Exact answer.

300 − 238 = 62

The customer should receive $62 in change.

8. A CD player at Flower Records costs $149. The same CD player at Bob's Dust Jacket costs $125. About how much more does the CD player cost at Flower Records?

Estimate.

150 − 130 = 20

The CD player costs about $ 20 more at Flower Records.

9. Tayonna bought a jacket for $24 and a shirt for $11. How much did she spend?

Exact answer.

24 + 11 = 35

Tayonna spent $ 35.

TEST-TAKING PRACTICE

Choose the best answer for each problem. In the answer section at the bottom of this page, fill in the box of your choice.

1. The stadium at the Ashland School seats 375 people. **If every game is sold out, about how many games will it take to sell 1,600 tickets?** D

   A 1 game C 3 games
   B 2 games D 4 games

2. Sylvia is making three shelves for her kitchen. One shelf is 16 inches long, another is 17 inches long, and the third is 18 inches long. If she cuts the 3 shelves from one board, what is the shortest length the board can be?

   What kind of answer do you need? K

   J an estimate
   K an exact answer
   L a money amount
   M a rounded-up number

3. Jackie bought a box of cards for $4.00. She gave the cashier a $10 bill. **How much change should she receive?** C

   A $4.00 C $6.00
   B $5.00 D $7.00

4. Mel makes $19 a week mowing lawns. **About how long will it take him to save $100?** M

   J 1 week L 4 weeks
   K 2 weeks M 5 weeks

5. The art museum had 819 visitors today. **If each visitor paid $6, about how much money did the museum take in?** C

   A $400 C $4,800
   B $800 D $5,400

Write About It

For this problem, decide whether you need an exact answer or an estimate. Then write a plan for solving the problem, and solve it.

6. **Charles wants to buy a pair of shoes for $50. He has $29 now. How much more money does he need to buy the shoes?**

   You need an exact answer.

   Subtract. 50 − 29 = 21. Charles needs $21 more to buy the shoes.

1. A ☐ B ☐ C ☐ D ☒
2. J ☐ K ☒ L ☐ M ☐
3. A ☐ B ☐ C ☒ D ☐
4. J ☐ K ☐ L ☐ M ☒
5. A ☐ B ☐ C ☒ D ☐

Name ______________________________

What Is the Question?

Some math problems that involve numbers ask for an answer that is not a number. Explaining a problem in your own words can help you identify the question you are being asked. It can also help you decide on the kind of answer you need.

Example 1

Jeremy grows fruit. He makes fresh-fruit baskets and sells them. For each basket, he needs 45 minutes to pick the fruit, clean it, and arrange it in the basket. A customer calls to order 7 baskets. The customer says she needs the baskets in 4 hours. Does Jeremy have enough time to fill the order?

A. Rewrite the question in your own words.

Is the time it takes Jeremy to make 7 baskets greater than or less than 4 hours? If it is greater, he cannot fill the order. If it is less, he can.

B. How much time does it take Jeremy to make 7 baskets?

45 x 7 = 305 minutes

C. Solve the problem that you wrote.

4 hours = 240 minutes

305 > 240

No, Jeremy does not have enough time to fill the order.

Example 2

Jeremy grows fruit. He makes fresh fruit-baskets and sells them. For each basket, he needs 45 minutes to pick the fruit, clean it, and arrange it in the basket. How long does it take Jeremy to make 2 baskets?

A. Is the answer to this question a number? yes

When a question asks for a number, you usually do not need to rewrite it.

B. Solve the problem.

2 x 45 = 90 **minutes**

So, it takes Jeremy 90 min **to make 2 baskets.**

GUIDED PRACTICE

1. Derrick is helping to raise money to build a new concert hall in his town. The Arts Committee has offered an award to anyone who raises $2,000. Derrick raised the following amounts over 4 weeks: $348, $750, $406, $813. Did Derrick raise enough money to earn an award?

   a. Is the answer to this question a number? no

   b. Rewrite the question in your own words.

   If the sum of the amounts that Derrick raised over 4 weeks is greater than or equal to $ 2,000 , he receives an award.

   c. Solve your problem.

   348 + 750 + 406 **+** 813 **=** 2,317

   Is the sum greater than or equal to $2,000? yes

   Answer the question.

   Yes, Derrick raised enough money to earn an award.

2. How much more would Derrick have to raise to earn a second award?

   a. Is the answer to this question a number? yes

   Even though this problem asks for an exact answer, you may still find it helpful to rewrite the question in your own words.

   b. Rewrite the question in your own words.

   How much more is the amount needed for 2 awards than the amount of money Derrick raised in 4 weeks?

   c. Solve your problem.

   4,000 **– 2,317 =** 1,683

   Answer the question.

   Derrck would have to raise $1,683 more to earn a second award.

PRACTICE

For problems 3 and 4, rewrite the question in your own words. Then solve.

3. Sam leaves work at 5:30 P.M. It takes him 1 hour and 15 minutes to edit 1 page. If it is 1:45 P.M., will he have time to edit 3 pages before he leaves?

Is the time it takes Sam to edit 3 pages less than or equal to the amount of time between 1:45 P.M. and 5:30 P.M.?

Will Sam have enough time to edit 3 pages before he leaves work?

yes

4. Adam plays harmonicas. He has harmonicas in 5 keys. If each harmonica cost $19.95, how much did it cost him to buy all 5?

What is the price of 5 harmonicas at $19.95 each?

It cost Adam $ 99.75 **to buy 5 harmonicas.**

Solve

5. A large office is moving. Each of the 80 people who work in the office has 2 boxes.

a. If the truck moving the boxes can take 30 boxes in one trip, will the boxes all be moved in 5 trips?

no

b. If it costs the company $15 to move each box, how much does the move cost in all?

$2,400

6. Liz and Ben are making a quilt. They need at least 5 yards of fabric. The fabric costs $25.67 a yard. Ben has $59, and Liz has $87.

a. Do they have enough money to buy the fabric they need?

yes

b. How much more money would Liz and Ben need to buy fabric for another quilt?

$110.70

TEST-TAKING PRACTICE

Choose the best answer for each problem. In the answer section at the bottom of this page, fill in the box of your choice.

1. Saul sells books. Each book costs him $4.95. He resells each book for $7.00. A customer wants to buy 150 books in bulk for a total of $742.50. Does Saul still make a profit?

   Which sentence is a way to rewrite the problem? B

   A The difference between $4.95 and $742.50 is the profit Saul makes.

   B If 150 times $4.95 is less than $742.50, Saul makes a profit.

   C If $742.50 divided by 150 is less than or equal to $4.95, Saul makes a profit.

   D The profit is $7.00 multiplied by 150.

2. A tall building has 14 steps from each floor to the next. **If Jannette walks 169 steps from the bottom floor will she make it to the 14th floor?** K

J yes	L 12.071
K no	M 155

3. Eduardo has averaged 1.92 goals per game over the last 3 seasons he has played soccer. **Going by his average, about how many goals should he score in 16 games?** B

A about 16	C about 36
B about 32	D about 48

Write About It

Rewrite the problem in your own words. Then solve.

4. **Mario makes patterns with tiles. In one pattern, he uses 5 orange squares, 3 white diamonds, and 4 green triangles. He has all the orange squares and white diamonds he needs. If Mario repeats the pattern 345 times, will 1,450 green triangles be enough?**

   If 345 times 4 is less than or equal to 1,450, Mario will have enough green triangles. 345 x 4 = 1,380, 1,380 < 1,450. So, 1,450 green triangles will be enough.

1. A ☐ B ☒ C ☐ D ☐

3. A ☐ B ☒ C ☐ D ☐

2. J ☐ K ☒ L ☐ M ☐

Underlining Information

Sometimes, a problem contains more information than you need. You can underline information in the problem to help you focus on the information you need to solve it.

Example

Camille takes people on walking tours. She visits interesting sites in the city where she lives. She takes a maximum of 8 people on each tour. The cost of the tour is $3.75 per person. Each tour takes 90 minutes. The tour goes to 6 places. The last stop on the tour is a chocolate factory. On Monday, 29 people sign up for tours. How many tours will Camille need to lead to provide a tour for everyone who signed up?

A. Read the problem carefully. Think about the question the problem asks. The question you need to answer is the last sentence:

How many tours will Camille need to lead to provide a tour for everyone who signed up?

Ring the question in the problem.

B. Now go back to the problem. What information do you need to answer the question?

She takes a maximum of 8 people on each tour.
On Monday, 29 people sign up for tours.

Underline the information that you need in the problem.

C. To find the number of tours, divide the number of people by the number on each tour.

29 ÷ 8 → 3 r5

The quotient means there are 3 groups of 8 people with 5 people left over.

So, to take all 29 people on tours, Camille must lead 4 **tours.**

GUIDED PRACTICE

Use the problems below to answer questions 1 and 2. They have the same information as the problem on page 25, but you need to underline different information to find the answers.

Version A

Camille takes people on walking tours. She visits interesting sites in the city where she lives. She takes a maximum of 8 people on each tour. The cost of the tour is $3.75 per person. Each tour takes 90 minutes. The tour goes to 6 places. The last stop on the tour is a chocolate factory. On Monday, 29 people sign up for tours.

Version B

Camille takes people on walking tours. She visits interesting sites in the city where she lives. She takes a maximum of 8 people on each tour. The cost of the tour is $3.75 per person. Each tour takes 90 minutes. The tour goes to 6 places. The last stop on the tour is a chocolate factory. On Monday, 29 people sign up for tours.

1. How much does Camille earn for one tour if the maximum number of people sign up for it?

   a. Which version has the information underlined that you need to solve this problem?

   Version B

   b. Solve the problem.

   8 x 3.75 **= $** 30.00

   So, Camille earns $ 30.00 **on one tour if the maximum number of people sign up for it.**

2. If the tour has 12 minutes walking time, how much time can be spent at each stop on the tour?

   a. Which version has the information underlined that you need to solve this problem?

   Version A

   b. Solve the problem.

   90 – 12 = 78 **minutes**

   78 ÷ 6 = 13 **minutes**

   So, 13 **minutes can be spent at each stop.**

Name ____________________

PRACTICE

Problems 3—6 use the same information. For each problem, ring the question you need to answer and underline the information you need to answer it.

3. Tim is reading a book about ancient Egypt. The book is 375 pages long. The book contains many photos of Egyptian art and architecture. Tim estimates that he reads 15 pages each night before he goes to bed. Someday he hopes to visit Egypt. He begins reading at 9:00 o'clock each evening.

   If he continues to read the book at the same rate, how many days will it take him to read the whole book?

   25 days

4. Tim is reading a book about ancient Egypt. The book is 375 pages long. The book contains many photos of Egyptian art and architecture. Tim estimates that he reads 15 pages each night before he goes to bed. Someday he hopes to visit Egypt. He begins reading at 9:00 o'clock each evening.

   If it takes Tim 5 minutes to read each page, at what time does he finish reading?

   10:15

5. Tim is reading a book about ancient Egypt. The book is 375 pages long. The book contains many photos of Egyptian art and architecture. Tim estimates that he reads 15 pages each night before he goes to bed. Someday he hopes to visit Egypt. He begins reading at 9:00 o'clock each evening.

   If a round-trip ticket to Egypt costs 3 times the number of pages in the book, how much does a round-trip ticket cost?

   $ 1,125

6. Tim is reading a book about ancient Egypt. The book is 375 pages long. The book contains many photos of Egyptian art and architecture. Tim estimates that he reads 15 pages each night before he goes to bed. Someday he hopes to visit Egypt. He begins reading at 9:00 o'clock each evening.

   If Tim finished reading tonight at 10:30, how long did it take him to read each page?

   6 **minutes**

TEST-TAKING PRACTICE

Use the information below to answer problems 1–3. Choose the best answer for each problem.

Jenna runs a business making deliveries by truck. One day she picks up a load of 120 crates of oranges to deliver to 3 different locations. She collects $5.35 for each crate that she delivers to a customer. The first delivery is to a grocery store. Jenna and her assistant take 23 minutes to unload 42 crates. The next delivery is to a fruit stand, and it takes 25 minutes. All but 30 crates are delivered. The final delivery takes 14 minutes.

1. How many crates are left after the second delivery is made?

   What information do you not need to answer the question? C

   A One day she picks up a load of 120 crates.

   B The first delivery is to a grocery store. She and her assistant take 23 minutes to unload 42 crates.

   C She collects $5.35 per crate that she delivers.

   D The next delivery is to a fruit stand and it takes 25 minutes. All but 30 crates are delivered.

2. **How much time in all did Jenna and her assistant spend unloading crates?** K

   J 48 min **L** 14 min
   K 62 min **M** 1 h

3. **What is the total amount of money Jenna collected from the second delivery?** C

   A $103.45 **C** $256.80
   B $220.10 **D** Not given

Write About It

In the problem at the top of the page, underline the information you need to answer this question. Write a plan for solving the problem, and then solve.

4. **How much longer did the first delivery take than the final delivery?**

   Subtract the time of the final delivery

   from the time of the first delivery.

   23 − 14 = 9 minutes. The first delivery

   took 9 minutes longer than the last

   delivery.

1. A ☐ B ☐ C ☒ D ☐
2. J ☐ K ☒ L ☐ M ☐
3. A ☐ B ☐ C ☒ D ☐

Name ____________________

Writing a Word Equation

When solving a multi-step word problem, you may find it helpful to explain the problem in your own words and write a word equation.

Example

Hattie and Murphy have collected 14 pounds of aluminum cans for a hospital fund-raiser. Each pound is worth $1.25. They want to raise a total of $20. How much more money do they need to raise?

A. Write a word equation to describe the problem.

Total money – Money collected = Money needed

Total money	Money collected	Money needed
↓	↓	↓
$20	**?**	**?**

B. You know the total ($20), but you don't know how much money Hattie and Murphy have already collected. Write a word equation to describe *just that part* of the question.

Pounds of cans	x	**Dollars per pound**	=	**Money collected**
↓		↓		↓
14	x	1.25	=	$ 17.50

C. You know the *pounds of cans* and the *money per pound* so you can solve the first equation.

Total Money	–	**Money collected**	=	**Money needed**
↓		↓		↓
20	–	17.50	=	$ 2.50

D. Answer the question:

Hattie and Murphy need to raise $ 2.50 **more.**

GUIDED PRACTICE

1. Josiah and Gabriel have collected 45 pounds of cardboard for a town fund-raiser. Each pound is worth $0.25. They want to raise $15. How much more money do they need to raise?

   a. Write a word equation to describe the problem.

   Total money – Money collected **= Money needed**

   b. Write a word equation describing the money already collected, and then solve it.

   Pounds of cardboard x Dollars per pound = Money collected

   45 x **$0.25** = $11.25

   c. You know the total money and the money collected, so you can solve the first equation and answer the question.

   Total money – Money collected **= Money needed**

   15 – 11.25 = 3.75

   So, Josiah and Gabriel need to raise $ 3.75 **more dollars.**

2. Josiah takes 10 pounds of cardboard to a recycling company that pays $0.25 per pound. Gabriel takes 15 pounds to another company that pays $0.40 a pound. How much more money than Josiah does Gabriel earn?

   a. Write a word equation to describe the problem.

   Money Gabriel earns **– Money Josiah earns = More money Gabriel earns**

   b. Solve.

   So, Gabriel earns $ 3.50 **more than Josiah.**

PRACTICE

The table below shows the amounts of different items found in a 100 pound sample of garbage. Use the table to answer the questions.

Different Items Found in Garbage (100 total pounds)

Item	Amount in pounds
paper products	38
food wastes	7
yard wastes	18
metals	8
glass	7
plastics	8
rubber, leather, textile, and wood	14

source: U.S. Environmental Protection Agency

3. How much heavier are the paper products than the combined weight of food and yard wastes? **Write word equations, and then solve.**

Weight of paper products – Combined weight of food and yard wastes = Greater weight of paper products.

Food wastes + yard wastes = Combined weight.

7 + 18 = 25 pounds. 38 – 25 = 13 pounds.

The weight of paper products is 13 **pounds greater than the combined weight of food and yard wastes.**

Solve

4. **How much heavier is the combined weight of rubber, leather, textile, wood, and plastics than the combined weight of metals and glass?**

The combined weight of rubber, leather, textile, wood, and plastics is 7 pounds heavier than the combined weight of metals and glass.

5. Suppose you doubled the amount of garbage in the sample by looking at a 200-pound sample of garbage. **How many pounds heavier would the metals be than the glass?**

The metals would weigh 2 pounds more than the glass in a 200-pound sample of garbage.

TEST-TAKING PRACTICE

Use the table to solve the problems. Choose the best answer for each problem.

Recycling Collections in Duncan

Recycling Item	Week 1	Week 2	Week 3
cans	345 lb	295 lb	298 lb
newspapers	576 lb	682 lb	598 lb
glass	259 lb	332 lb	416 lb
plastics	132 lb	137 lb	281 lb

1. For Week 1, the amount of nonrecyclable garbage was half the weight of the cans and newspapers combined. How heavy was the nonrecyclable garbage?

   Which equation could not be used to solve the problem? D

   A weight of cans + weight newspapers = weight of cans and newspapers combined.
   B weight of cans and newspapers combined ÷ 2 = weight of nonrecyclable garbage.
   C 345 + 576 = 921 pounds
   D 345 ÷ 2 = weight of nonrecyclable garbage.

2. **How much more plastic was collected during Week 3 than the combined total amount collected in Week 1 and Week 2?** K

   J 5 lb **L** 149 lb
   K 12 lb **M** 269 lb

3. **How many more pounds of recyclables were collected in Week 2 than in Week 1?** C

   A 110 lb **C** 134 lb
   B 132 lb **D** 137 lb

Write About It

Write word equations for solving the problem, and then solve.

4. **How much more newspaper was collected in Week 2 than the total amount of plastics collected in all three weeks combined?**

   Newspaper collected in Week 2 – plastics from all 3 weeks = how much more newspaper. Plastic from weeks 1 + 2 + 3 = combined pounds of plastic. 132 + 137 + 281 = 550. 682 – 550 = 132 pounds. So, 132 more pounds of newspaper were collected.

1. A ☐ B ☐ C ☐ D ☒ 3. A ☐ B ☐ C ☒ D ☐
2. J ☐ K ☒ L ☐ M ☐

Name ______________________________ **Chapters 1–2**

Test-Taking Skill: Writing a Plan

Some questions on tests ask you to explain how you solve a problem. Write a plan to show the steps you take. Show your calculations.

Example 1

Population of Midland City

Year	Population
1853	207,089
1860	813,669
1995	7,322,564

How many more people lived in Midland City in 1860 than in 1835?

A. **Read the problem carefully. Decide on the kind of answer you need.**

The answer called for is the difference between a city's population in 1860 and in 1835.

B. **Write a plan for finding the answer**. First, I will look in the second column of the table to find the population figures. Then, I will subtract to find the difference.

C. **Follow your plan, and answer the question.**

Population in 1860 – Population in 1835 = Difference in population

813,669 – 207,089 = 606,580

A total of 606,580 **more people lived in Midland City in 1860 than in 1835.**

Example 2

Was the population growth in Midland City greater between 1835 and 1860 or between 1860 and 1995?

A. **Decide on the kind of answer you need, and write a plan.**
I need to find the time interval in which the difference in population was greater. I already found the difference for the time interval between 1835 and 1860 in **Example 1.** I will have to find the difference for the time interval between 1860 and 1995 and then compare the two differences.

B. **Follow the plan, and answer the question.**

Population difference from 1835 to 1860: 606,580

Population difference from 1860 to 1995: 7,322,564 – 813,669 = 6,508,695

6,508,695 > 606,580

So, the population growth from 1860 to 1995 was greater **than the population growth between 1835 and 1860.**

TEST-TAKING PRACTICE

Public Libraries Systems		
City	Population Served	Number of Books
Los Angeles, California	3,681,708	5,743,103
San Antonio, Texas	1,310,500	1,754,291
Toronto, Ontario	637,049	2,087,863
Detroit, Michigan	1,027,974	2,804,428

Use the table. Write a plan to solve each problem. Follow your plan, and solve.

1. How many people does the library with the fewest books serve? Which city is it in?

Look in the third column (number of books) for the lowest number. Then read across to find the population number in the second column and the name of the city in the first column. The lowest number in the third column is 1,754,291. The library serves 1,310,500 people and is in San Antonio.

2. How many more people are served by the library system that serves the largest population than the one that serves the smallest population? Name the systems.

Read the table to find the library system that serves the largest population and the one that serves the smallest population. Then subtract to find the difference between them.

Los Angeles serves the largest population with 3,681,708; and Toronto serves the smallest population with 637,049.

Subtract : 3,681,708 – 637,049 = 3,044,659

The Los Angeles library system serves 3,044,659 more people than the Toronto library system.

Using Simpler Numbers

Sometimes, using simpler numbers can help you to solve a problem.

The table below shows the numbers of calories used during different exercises by a person who weighs 100 pounds.

Calories Used During Exercises

Activity	Calories Used Per Minute
walking	2.7
jogging	6.1
volleyball	2.3

Example 1

Dale weighs 100 pounds. Each morning, she walks for 25 minutes. How many calories does she use each morning? Use the information in the table.

A. You can use simpler numbers to plan how to solve the problem.

Exact Number	**Simpler Number**
2.7	**3**

B. Next, use a simpler number to set up the problem.

25 x 3 = 75

Now, you can use the exact number to find the exact answer.

25 **x 2.7 =** 67.5

So, Dale uses 67.5 **calories each morning.**

Example 2

Armand weighs 100 pounds. He used 103.5 calories playing volleyball. For how many minutes did he play?

A. Use simpler numbers to set up and solve the problem.

104 ÷ 2 = 52

B. Now, use the exact numbers to find the exact answer.

103.5 ÷ 2.3 = 45

So, Armand played volleyball for 45 **minutes.**

GUIDED PRACTICE

The table below shows the numbers of calories used during different exercises by a person who weighs 100 pounds.

Calories Used During Exercises

Activity	Calories Used Per Minute
walking	2.7
jogging	6.1
volleyball	2.3

1. Aziz weighs 100 pounds. He jogged for 15 minutes and then walked for 12 more minutes. How many calories did he use?

   a. Use simpler numbers to help you solve the problem.

   For jogging, 6.1 simplifies to 6.

   For walking, __2.7__ **simplifies to** __3__.

   b. Use the simpler numbers to set up and solve the problem.

   15 x __6__ = __90__ **calories**

   __12__ x __3__ = __36__ **calories**

   Add.

   __90__ + __36__ = __126__ **calories**

   Now, use the exact numbers to find the exact answer.

   15 x __6.1__ = __91.5__ **calories**

   __12__ x __2.7__ = __32.4__ **calories**

   __91.5__ + __32.4__ = __123.9__ **calories**

   So, Aziz used __123.9__ **calories during his exercise.**

2. Aziz pays $2.25 an hour to use the Sports Center. He was there for 3 hours a day for 5 days last week. How much did he pay for the week? **Use simpler numbers to plan the problem. Then find the exact answer.**

   First, multiply to find how many hours he was there.

   __3__ x __5__ = __15__ **hours**

   Then, use simpler numbers to solve the problem.

   __15__ x __2__ = __30__ **dollars**

   Now, use the exact numbers to find the exact answer.

   __15__ x __2.25__ = __33.75__ **dollars**

   So, Aziz paid $ __33.75__ **for the week.**

Name ______________________________

PRACTICE

Janira is a buyer for a restaurant. The table below shows the price per pound of various items that she needs to buy for the party. Use the table to solve the problems.

Market Prices

Item	Price Per Pound
Leg of Lamb	$9.83
Iceberg Lettuce	$2.29
New Potatoes	$3.79
T-Bone Steak	$12.32
Pork Chops	$9.03

For problems 3 and 4, use simpler numbers to plan. Then solve exactly.

3. Janira decided to buy an 8-pound leg of lamb. How much will the lamb cost?

   9.83 simplifies to 10. 10 x 8 = 80

   9.83 x 8 = 78.64

   The lamb will cost $ 78.64.

4. Janira paid $16.45 for a 5-pound bag of new potatoes on sale. What was the sale price per pound?

   16.45 simplifies to 16. 16 ÷ 5 = 3.2

   16.45 ÷ 5 = 3.29

   The sale price was $ 3.29.

Solve . . . .

5. Janira decided to buy 12 pounds of pork chops and 9 pounds of T-bone steak. **How much did Janira pay for these items?**

   Janira paid $219.24.

6. Janira paid $9.45 for 5 pounds of iceberg lettuce on sale. **How much less was the sale price per pound than the regular price per pound?**

   The sale price was $0.40 less.

7. Just before leaving the market, Janira saw a 9-pound leg of lamb on sale for $80.91. **How much was its price per pound?**

   Its price per pound was $8.99.

8. Janira decided to buy 4 more pounds of potatoes and 5 more pounds of lettuce at regular prices. **How much did she have to pay?**

   She had to pay $26.61.

TEST-TAKING PRACTICE

Use the information in the table to answer questions 1–4. Choose the best answer for each problem. In the answer section at the bottom of this page, fill in the box of your choice.

Swimming Times

Swimmer	Time for One Lap
Chris	23.56 s
Marna	24.77 s
Kathy	21.07 s

1. Which would be good simpler numbers for the three times? D

A Chris 23 s, Marna 24 s, Kathy 21 s

B Chris 23.6 s, Marna 24.8 s, Kathy 21.1 s

C Chris 23.5 s, Marna 24.7 s, Kathy 21.0 s

D Chris 24 s, Marna 25 s, Kathy 21 s

2. Which operation will tell you which swimmer swam 4 laps at lap time in 84.28 s? K

J Divide each time by 4.

K Divide 84.28 by each time.

L Multiply each time by 84.28.

M Subtract each time from 84.28.

3. At his lap time, how long would it take Chris to swim 5 laps? C

A 4.71 s C 117.8 s

B 23.56 s D 120 s

4. The clock shows 63.21 s. How many laps did Kathy swim? K

J 21.07 s L 4

K 3 M 6

Write About It

Write a plan to solve the problem by using simpler numbers. Then find the exact answer by using the actual numbers from the table. Explain how you found your answers.

5. Marna and Chris swam laps as a team. They each swam 3 laps. What was their combined time?

First, simplify the numbers.

Multiply, and then add.

24 x 3 = 72 25 x 3 = 75

72 + 75 = 147

For the exact answer, use the

numbers from the table.

23.56 x 3 = 70.68

24.77 x 3 = 74.31

Their combined time was 144.99 s.

1. A ☐ B ☐ C ☐ D ☒ 3. A ☐ B ☐ C ☒ D ☐

2. J ☐ K ☒ L ☐ M ☐ 4. J ☐ K ☒ L ☐ M ☐

Name ____________________

Underlining Information

Sometimes, you might find it helpful to underline the information you need to solve a problem.

Example 1

Tickets to a football game cost $8 for adults and $5.75 for students. Children under 5 can go for free. What is the cost of 6 student tickets?

A. What is the question that you have to answer?

What is the cost of 6 student tickets?

B. Look at the problem again, and find the information you need to answer the question. Underline the information.

$5.75 for students

C. Use the information that you underlined to answer the question.

6 x 5.75 = 34.50

So, the cost of 6 student tickets is $ 34.50 **.**

Example 2

Two of the world's fastest animals are the greyhound and the cheetah. The greyhound is a racing dog and weighs about 65 pounds. The fastest recorded speed of a greyhound is 39.35 miles per hour. The cheetah weighs about 100 pounds and feeds on small deer and antelopes. To catch its prey, a cheetah can reach a speed of 70 miles per hour. Can a cheetah run twice as fast as a greyhound?

Step 1: Underline the information you need to answer the question.

Step 2: Use the information you underlined to answer the question.

You can use estimation to compare the numbers.

THINK: Round 39.35 to the nearest ten. So, a greyhound can run at about 40 miles per hour.

Find twice the estimated speed of a greyhound. 2 x 40 = 80

Compare the two numbers. 80 > **70**

Can a cheetah run twice as fast as a greyhound? no

GUIDED PRACTICE

1. Dominic worked at a video store on Saturday. He sold 23 videos, rented 85 videos, and 12 laser discs. He earned $26.25 for 5 hours of work. How much was he paid per hour?

   a. Underline the information you need to answer the question.

   b. Use the information that you underlined to answer the question.

   26.25 **÷ 5 =** 5.25

   So, Dominic was paid $ 5.25 **per hour.**

2. The whippet is a dog that looks like a greyhound, but the whippet is much smaller. A whippet weighs about 20 pounds. The fastest recorded speed of a whippet is 35.50 miles per hour, but whippets are not often raced. Greyhounds, on the other hand, are known as racing dogs. A greyhound can reach a speed of 39.35 miles per hour. How much faster can a greyhound run than a whippet?

   a. Underline the information you need to answer the question.

   b. Use the information that you underlined to answer the question.

   39.35 **– 35.50 =** 3.85

   The greyhound can run 3.85 **miles an hour faster than the whippet.**

Name ______________________________

PRACTICE

For problems 3 and 4, underline the information you need. Then solve.

3. Diana loves animals and researches them as a hobby. She looked up horses in the encyclopedia and found that their top speed is 47.5 miles per hour. The next day she rode her horse 18.5 miles in 2 hours. How many miles did Diana ride per hour?

18.5 ÷ 2 = 9.25

Diana rode 9.25 miles per hour.

4. Track is a popular sport at the Chavez School. There are 27 boys and girls on the track team. The team trains on a track that is 0.25 miles around. Each night, the team trains for 2 hours. If the team members run 24 laps, how many miles have they run?

24 x 0.25 = 6

The team members have run 6 miles.

Solve . . . .

5. Talitha and 2 friends share a paper route with 212 customers. This month they received the following tips: $11.89, $9.87, and $8.78. If they share the tips equally, how much money will each person receive?

11.89 + 9.87 + 8.78 = 30.54

30.54 ÷ 3 = 10.18; each person

will receive $10.18.

6. Levar and Andrew are training for a walking race. Levar has been training for 10 months and can walk at 5 miles per hour. Andrew walks at 4 miles per hour. The race is 2 miles long. How long will it take Levar to finish the race?

2 ÷ 5 = 0.4; Levar will finish the

race in 0.4 of an hour.

7. A ferry boat service on Blue Mountain Lake takes passengers across the lake for $6.50 each. Each trip is one-way only. The lake is 3.4 miles across. If the ferry makes 18 trips a day, how many miles does it travel?

18 x 3.4 = 61.2; the ferry travels

61.2 miles per day.

8. For a reunion, the Proctor family rented a cottage for $3,000 for one week. Family members also shared the food bill, which came to $489.78. The Proctor family has 5 members. About how much did each person pay for the vacation?

3,000 + 500 = 3,500; 3,500 ÷ 5= 700

Each person paid about $700.

TEST-TAKING PRACTICE

Use the information below for problems 1–3. Choose the best answer for each problem. In the answer section at the bottom of this page, fill in the box of your choice.

A class at Webster School collected data on ball-throwing distances. They found that the average distance a Webster student can throw a ball is 15 yards. Some students can throw the ball much farther, and some can't throw it as far. A student named Henry threw the ball 1.5 times the average throw. Tara threw the ball only 0.75 times the average.

1. How far did Tara throw the ball? **Which information should you underline to help to answer this question?** B
   - **A** The students at Webster School collected data on ball-throwing distances.
   - **B** The average student at Webster School can throw a ball 15 yards.
   - **C** Some students can throw the ball much farther.
   - **D** Henry threw the ball 1.5 times the average throw.

2. **How far did Henry throw the ball?** L
   - **J** 1.5 yd
   - **K** 15 yd
   - **L** 22.5 yd
   - **M** 225 yd

3. **If Jenna threw the ball 3.2 yards farther than 15 yards, how far did she throw it?** C
   - **A** 3.2 yd
   - **B** 15 yd
   - **C** 18.2 yd
   - **D** 48 yd

Write About It

In the problem below, underline the information you need to answer it. Explain why you didn't underline some of the information. Then solve.

A sample answer is given.

4. Boise, Idaho, whose metropolitan area is 1,060 square miles, has an average daily high temperature in January of 36.4°F. Honolulu, Hawaii, whose metropolitan area is 621 square miles, has an average daily high temperature in January of 80.1°F. **Is Honolulu's average daily high temperature in January more than twice that of Boise's?**

You don't underline the parts about the metropolitan areas because they are not needed for the problem.

$36.4 \times 2 = 72.8$; $72.8 < 80.1$

So, 80.1°F is more than twice 36.4°F. Honolulu's average daily high temperature in January is more than twice that of Boise's.

1. A ☐ B ☒ C ☐ D ☐
2. J ☐ K ☐ L ☒ M ☐
3. A ☐ B ☐ C ☒ D ☐

Name ______________________

Interpreting the Quotient

Carefully reading the question in a division problem will help you decide on the kind of answer you need and how to interpret the quotient.

Here are three problems you can solve with the same number sentence.

1. The workers at a factory take 18 seconds to stamp a logo on each product. How many logos can they stamp on products in 45 seconds?
2. A shuttle-bus service takes people from a hotel to a train station. Each bus can carry 18 people. One day, 45 people are waiting to take the shuttle. How many buses are needed?
3. Zane is organizing a camping trip. He needs 18 short pieces of rope of equal length to set up the tents. He has 1 piece of rope that is 45 feet long. If he cuts the rope into 18 equal pieces, how long will each piece be?

You can use this number sentence for each problem:

45 ÷ 18 = 2.5

The numbers are the same, but they mean something different in each problem.

	45 ÷	18 =	2.5
1.	Total time	Time per logo	The workers can stamp on 2.5 logos in 45 seconds.
2.	People waiting	People per bus	To take 45 people, 2.5 buses are needed.
3.	Length of rope	Pieces of rope	Zane can cut 45 feet of rope into 18 pieces 2.5 feet long.

Problem 1: **Because it does not make sense to stamp on only part of a logo, the answer to the question is __2__ logos.**

Problem 2: **Because the answer "2.5 buses" does not make sense, the answer to the question is __3__ buses.**

Problem 3: **Because 2.5 feet is a measurement, the answer to the question is __2.5__ feet.**

GUIDED PRACTICE

Complete each chart to answer each problem.

Problem-Solving Tips:
To solve a division problem whose quotient is a decimal, you may need to

- round down to the nearest whole number.
- round up to the nearest whole number.
- use the exact answer.

1. Jose coaches an elementary school soccer team. The team has a budget of $450 for jerseys. Each jersey costs $40. How many jerseys can Jose buy?

450	÷ 40	= 11.25
Team budget	Cost of jersey	Number of jerseys Jose can buy

What does the quotient mean?

Jose can buy 11 full jerseys and 0.25 of another jersey.

So, Jose can buy 11 **jerseys.**

2. Tanya is hiking a trail that is 450 kilometers long. Each day, she hikes 40 kilometers. How many days will it take Tanya to hike the entire trail?

450	÷ 40	= 11.25
Length of trail in kilometers	Kilometers Tanya hikes each day	Number of days Tanya hikes

What does the quotient mean?

After hiking for 11 days, she still has to hike another 0.25 day to finish the trail.

So, it will take 12 **days for Tanya to hike the trail.**

3. Kim makes earrings and sells them to jewelry stores. One store orders 40 pairs of earrings for a total of $450. What is the cost to the store for 1 pair of earrings?

450	÷ 40	= 11.25
Total cost for earrings	Number of pairs of earrings	Cost of one pair of earrings

So, the cost to the store for 1 pair of earrings is $ 11.25**.**

Name ____________________ **Chapter 3** L3

PRACTICE

For each problem, tell what the quotient means. Then complete the answer.

4. Stevie is planning a family reunion. He needs to find out how many picnic tables he will need. He expects 46 people to attend. Each picnic table seats 8 people. How many picnic tables will Stevie need?

   What does the quotient mean?

   If each table holds 8 people,

   46 people will fill 5.75 tables.

   So, Stevie will need 6 **picnic tables.**

5. Eight friends decide to share a large order of chicken wings. A large order has 53 wings. They decide to share the wings evenly and save whatever is left for a ninth friend who's coming later. How many wings can each of the 8 friends have?

   What does the quotient mean?

   Each of the 8 friends can

   have 6.625 wings.

   So, each of the 8 friends can have 6 **chicken wings.**

Solve

6. Ancient Romans measured length using a unit called a *cubit*. A Roman cubit is 17.5 inches long. **About how many feet are there in 1 cubit?**

   There are about 1.5 feet in a cubit.

7. Aza is planning a canoe trip for 25 people. Each canoe can hold 2 people. **How many canoes will Aza need?**

   Aza will need 13 canoes.

8. Siva makes computers. Each computer has 36 chips in it. **If Siva has 306 computer chips, how many computers can she make?**

   Siva can make 8 computers.

9. Esmerelda buys 4 CDs for $25. **If each CD costs the same amount of money, how much does 1 CD cost?**

   One CD costs $6.25.

10. In a video game, Bernardo races a car around a track 5 times. His total time is 3 minutes and 26 seconds. **To a tenth of a second, what is his average time per lap?**

    His average time per lap is 41.2 seconds.

11. Ryan is recording some songs. **If each song is 2 minutes and 30 seconds long, how many songs can Ryan record on a 60-minute tape?**

    Ryan can record 24 songs.

TEST-TAKING PRACTICE

Choose the best answer for each problem. Then in the answer section at the bottom of this page, fill in the box of your choice.

1. A town baseball league is going to the So Much Fun amusement park. It will cost $11 for each person to go. The league has 484 people in it. If each bus seats 40 people, how many buses will the league need?

   What does the decimal in the quotient mean in this problem? B

   A Some people will not go to the amusement park.
   B Some people will go to the amusement park on a bus that is not full.
   C A fraction of a bus will go to the amusement park.
   D The amount of change each person will get if he or she pays with a $20 bill.

2. Darlene is organizing a running race. The course is 8 miles long. She wants to break the race up into 5 equal sections.

   To the nearest tenth of a mile, how long is each section of the race? L

   J 1.0 mile **L** 1.6 miles
   K 1 R2 miles **M** 2.0 miles

3. Dale makes model cars. He needs 5 wheels for each car because each has a spare tire.

   If Dale has 153 wheels, how many cars can he make? A

   A 30 **C** 30.6
   B 30 R2 **D** 31

4. Juan is the captain of the chess club at his school. He has to buy chess sets for the chess club with money from the school budget. With $250.00, he buys 14 sets.

   How much does each set cost? M

   J $17 **L** $17.80
   K 17 R12 **M** Not given

Write About It

5. At the store, Mark wants to buy as many grapes as he can with $18.60. Grapes cost $2.00 a pound. To the nearest tenth of a pound, how many pounds can Mark buy?

   Find the quotient. What does the decimal stand for? Do you need to round? Solve.

   18.60 ÷ 2.00 = 9.3. The decimal is a fraction of a pound. Because 9.3 is an exact answer, you do not need to round. So, Mark can buy 9.3 pounds of grapes.

1. A ☐ B ☒ C ☐ D ☐
2. J ☐ K ☐ L ☒ M ☐
3. A ☒ B ☐ C ☐ D ☐
4. J ☐ K ☐ L ☐ M ☒

Name ____________________

Which Answer Makes Sense?

Deciding on the kind of answer you need will help you to solve problems. Sometimes, you have to decide whether or not you need to round your answer.

Example 1

Sang wants to send gift cards to some of his family members who live in Korea. He has $15.00 to spend. The gift cards he likes cost $4.00 each. How many cards can Sang buy?

A. You want to know how many gift cards Sang can buy with $15.00. You can divide $15.00 by $4.00 to find the answer.

$$15.00 \div 4.00 = 3.75$$

B. Look at the question you need to answer:

How many cards can Sang buy?

Notice that the question asks how many cards rather than how much something costs.

The number 3.75 tells you that $15.00 is enough money for more than 3 gift cards but not enough for 4. You cannot buy a part of a card. You need to round the number down to 3.

So, Sang can buy 3 cards.

Example 2

Sang finds 9 postcards that he likes and buys them. Each postcard costs $0.75. What is the total cost of the postcards?

Step 1: You know that each postcard costs $0.75 and that Sang buys 9 cards. You can multiply to find the total cost.

$$9 \times 0.75 = 6.75$$

Step 2: Look at the question you need to answer:

What is the total cost of the postcards?

The answer should be a money amount. You do not need to round it because you can write money amounts with two decimal places.

So, the total cost of the postcards is $ 6.75 .

GUIDED PRACTICE

Use the prices in the window display to solve each problem.

1. A 1-pound bag of apples contains 4 apples. Alexa wants to buy only one apple. What would be the cost of one apple?

   a. You want to know the cost of one apple when 4 apples cost $1.10. You can divide.

   1.10 ÷ __4__ = 0.275

   b. Decide on the kind of answer you need.

   > Note: Stores always round up 0.5.

   Should the answer be a money amount? __Yes__

   Does 0.275 answer the question? __No__

   Does the answer need to be rounded to make sense? __Yes__

   What is the answer that makes sense? $ __0.28__

   So, one apple costs $ __0.28__**.**

2. Delia needs to buy chicken for a barbecue. She has $13.50 to spend. How many pounds of chicken can she buy?

   a. You want to know how many times $2.00 goes into $13.50. You can divide.

   __13.50__ ÷ __2.00__ **= 6.75**

   b. Decide on the kind of answer you need.

   Should the answer be a money amount? __No__

   Should the answer be rounded? __No__

   What is the answer that makes sense? __6.75__ **pounds of chicken**

   So, Delia can buy __6.75__ **pounds of chicken.**

Name ______________________________

PRACTICE

For problems 3 and 4, write whether each answer should be a money amount and whether it should be rounded. Then solve.

3. Mr. Bertram wants to rent a car to visit his relatives in Boston. The car rental company charges $49.98 per day. The trip will last 3 days. How much will it cost to rent the car?

The answer should be a money amount,

and it does not have to be rounded.

It will cost Mr. Bertram

$ 149.94 to rent the car for 3 days.

4. Gillian wants to see a movie. A regular ticket costs $3.75. The theater is offering half-price tickets for the weekday matinee. How much will a matinee ticket cost?

The answer should be a money amount,

and it does have to be rounded.

A matinee ticket will cost

$1.88 .

Solve

5. A bicycle race is divided into 5 legs. Each leg is 4.65 miles long. **What is the total length of the race?**

The race is 23.25 miles long

6. Jorge likes to make model airplanes. He has $100.00, and each model kit costs $12.98. Jorge calculates this answer: 7.70. **How many model kits can he buy?**

Jorge can buy 7 model-airplane kits.

7. Joplin works at a bakery. In 8 hours, she bakes 420 rolls. **To the nearest 10 rolls, about how many rolls does she bake each hour?**

She bakes about 50 rolls an hour

8. Fiona spends a lot of time on the Internet. She pays $29.78 a month for her Internet service. **How much does she spend for Internet service for a year?**

Fiona spends $357.36 for a year.

TEST-TAKING PRACTICE

Choose the best answer for each problem. In the answer section at the bottom of this page, fill in the box of your choice.

Use the information in the table to answer questions 1-4.

Prices at Sports City

Item	Price
running shoes	$37.55
sweat socks	$1.29
sweat pants	$21.90
sweat shirt	$9.00

1. Renata wants to buy a sweat shirt for each of her 3 children. **How much must she spend to buy the sweat shirts?** C

   A $9.00 C $27.00
   B $18.00 D $36.00

2. Malcolm wants to buy sweat pants for his soccer team. **How many pairs of sweat pants can he buy with $350.00?** J

   J 15 L 15.98
   K $15.98 M 16

3. Frank wants to buy matching sweat pants and sweat shirts for the 9 members of his baseball team. **How much must he spend to buy the sets of sweat pants and sweat shirts?** B

   A $30.90 C $300.90
   B $278.10 D $378.10

Write About It

Write a plan for solving the problem. Will the answer be a money amount? Will you need to round? Solve.

4. **Mrs. Jenkins wants to buy a pair of running shoes and a pair of socks for each of her grandchildren. If she has $250.00, how many sets of shoes and socks can she buy.**

Add the prices for running shoes ($37.55) and sweat socks ($1.29). Then divide $250.00 by that number. The answer will not be a money amount, and you will need to round. $37.55 + $1.29 = $38.84, $250.00 ÷ $38.84 = 6.436. 6.436 rounded down = 6. She can buy 6 sets.

1. A ❑ B ❑ C ☒ D ❑
2. J ☒ K ❑ L ❑ M ❑
3. A ❑ B ☒ C ❑ D ❑

Name ______________________________

Solving Multi-Step Problems

Sometimes, you may need to take three or more steps to solve a problem. To solve such problems, it is helpful to decide what you can find first.

Example

The town council is having a bake sale. So far, the council has sold 9 brownies for $0.50 each and 14 cookies for $0.35 each. How much has the council earned so far?

A. You need to find the total earned. You can write a word equation to show the problem.

Money earned selling brownies + **Money earned selling cookies** = **Total earned**

B. Look at the word equation. Decide what you can find first.

Before you add, you have to know which numbers to add.

To find the numbers, first find out how much the council earned selling brownies and how much the council earned selling cookies.

Money earned selling brownies = 9 x 0.50 → **$** 4.50

Money earned selling cookies = 14 x 0.35 → **$** 4.90

C. Put the numbers you found into the word equation you wrote. Then solve.

Money earned selling brownies + **Money earned selling cookies** = **Total earned**

↓ ↓ ↓

4.50 + 4.90 = $ 9.40

So, the town council has earned $ 9.40 **so far.**

GUIDED PRACTICE

1. At the bake sale, Christie buys 3 cookies and 2 brownies. She pays with a $5 bill. What change should she receive?

Step 1: Write a word equation to find Christie's change from a $5 bill.

$5 – Amount spent = Christie's change

Step 2: Write a word equation to find the amount spent.

Cost of 2 brownies + Cost of 3 cookies **= Amount spent**

Step 3: Find the numbers to put in the word equation.

Cost of 2 brownies	+	**Cost of 3 cookies**	=	Amount spent
↓		↓		↓
$1.00	+	$ 1.05	=	$ 2.05

Step 4: Look at the first word equation.
Write the numbers you now know in the equation. Then solve.

$ 5	–	**Amount spent**	=	**Christie's change**
↓		↓		↓
$ 5	–	$ 2.05	=	$ 2.95

So, Christie gets $ 2.95 **in change from a $5 bill.**

2. The head baker estimated that each brownie cost $0.20 to make. By the end of the day, the town council had sold 245 brownies at $0.50 each. How much did the council make on brownies?

Step 1: Write a word equation to find the profit made selling brownies.

Amount made selling brownies – Amount spent making brownies = Amount made on brownies

Step 2: Write word equations to find numbers for the first word equation. Then solve.

Amount made selling brownies = Number of brownies sold x Cost of a brownie → $0.50 x 245 = $122.50. Amount spent making brownies = Number of brownies sold x Cost to make a brownie → 245 x $0.20 = $49.00. 122.50 – 49.00 = $73.50.

So, the town council made $ 73.50 **on brownies.**

Name ______________________________

PRACTICE

For problems 3 and 4, write word equations to help you decide what to do first and how to solve the problem. Then solve.

3. The town soccer team sold pizzas to raise money. The team members sold 24 cheese pizzas at $11.50 each and 37 sausage pizzas at $13.75 each. What was the total earned?

Word equations:

Word equations may vary. Check students' work.

The total earned was $ 784.75.

4. Jordan bought 7 pizzas for $11.50 each and 4 pizzas for $13.75 each. He gave the delivery person $140. What change should he receive?

Word equations:

Word equations may vary. Check students' work.

Jordan should receive $ 4.50.

Solve . . . .

5. The pizza company can make 12 pizzas an hour. If the company makes pizzas for 8 hours, its costs are $395.52. **How much does it cost the company to make one pizza?**

It costs the pizza company $4.12 to make one pizza.

6. The swim team sold 87 pizzas for a total of $1,095. The team can keep $3.50 for each pizza. The rest of the money is paid to the pizza company. **How much money does the team owe the pizza company?**

The team owes the pizza company $790.50.

TEST-TAKING PRACTICE

Choose the best answer for each problem. In the answer section at the bottom of the page, fill in the box of your choice.

1. Bella bought 12 roses for $1.50 each and 18 carnations for $0.98 each. She gave the flower shop $40. What change should she receive?

   Which equation could help you decide what to do first in this problem? A

   A $40 – the total cost of the flowers = the change Bella should receive.
   B 12 x 1.50 = the change Bella should receive.
   C 18 + 12 = $30 + the change Bella should receive.
   D $40 – the cost of one flower = the change Bella should receive.

2. **Anne worked for three hours. Her pay was three $5 bills, two $1 bills, and one quarter. How much did she earn per hour?** K

   J $5.50 L $15.75
   K $5.75 M $17.75

3. **Kinte bought 2 shirts for $9.95 each, 1 pair of pants for $25.99, and 4 pairs of socks for $3.49 each. How much did he spend?** D

   A $19.90 C $49.38
   B $45.89 D $59.85

4. **Zoe sold 37 posters for $8.95 each, 18 photographs for $5.00 each, and 20 postcards for $0.25 each. What is the total of her sales?** L

   J $331.15 L $426.15
   K $421.15 M $471.15

Write About It

Write a plan for solving the following problem. Then solve.

5. **Vinnie rents 3 video games at $3.59 each and 2 movies at $2.95 each. He gives the clerk a $20 bill. How much change should he receive?**

   Answers will vary. Sample answer given. **Plan:** Write a word equation to show the problem. Decide what to do first. Then solve the problem. **Solution:** $20 – (3 video games at $3.59 each + 2 movies at $2.95 each) = Vinnie's cost. $20 – ($10.77 + $5.90) = Vinnie's change: $3.33.

1. A ☒ B ☐ C ☐ D ☐
2. J ☐ K ☒ L ☐ M ☐
3. A ☐ B ☐ C ☐ D ☒
4. J ☐ K ☐ L ☒ M ☐

Name ______________________________

Writing an Equivalent Problem

Showing the information in a problem in a different way can sometimes help you solve the problem. One way of doing this is to write an equivalent problem.

Example 1

Community theater members sold dried fruit for \$3 per pound. They earned a total of \$813.75. How many pounds of dried fruit did they sell?

A. You can write a word equation that shows the problem's information.

Total money earned = Dollars per pound x Number of pounds

B. You can write an equivalent division equation from the first equation. The question asks how many pounds the theater sold. So, you need to write an equation for the **number of pounds.**

Total money earned ÷ Dollars per pound = Number of pounds

C. Write the numbers you know into the equation, and then solve.

813.75 ÷ 3 **=** 271.25 **pounds**

So, the community theater sold 271.25 **pounds of dried fruit.**

Example 2

Roxanne is a goalie on the local hockey team. She makes an average of 12.5 saves per game. If the team played 26 games in the season, how many total saves did Roxanne make?

Step 1: You can write a word equation that shows the problem's information.

Average saves per game = Total saves **÷ Number of games**

Step 2: You can write an equivalent multiplication equation from the equation above. The question asks how many total saves Roxanne made. So, you need to write an equation for the **total saves.**

Number of games **x** Average saves per game **= Total saves**

Step 3: Write the numbers you know into the equation, and then solve.

26 x 12.5 **=** 325 **saves**

So, Roxanne made a total of 325 **saves.**

GUIDED PRACTICE

1. A group of Boy Scouts sold baseball caps for $3.00 each at the city softball championships. They earned a total of $870.00. How many baseball caps did they sell?

   a. Write a word equation that shows the problem's information.

   Total money earned = Price per cap **x** Number of caps sold

   b. Write an equivalent division equation for the number of caps sold.

   Total money earned ÷ Price per cap **= Number of caps sold**

   c. Write the numbers you know into the equation, and then solve.

   870 ÷ 3 = 290 **caps sold**

   So, the Boy Scouts sold a total of 290 **baseball caps.**

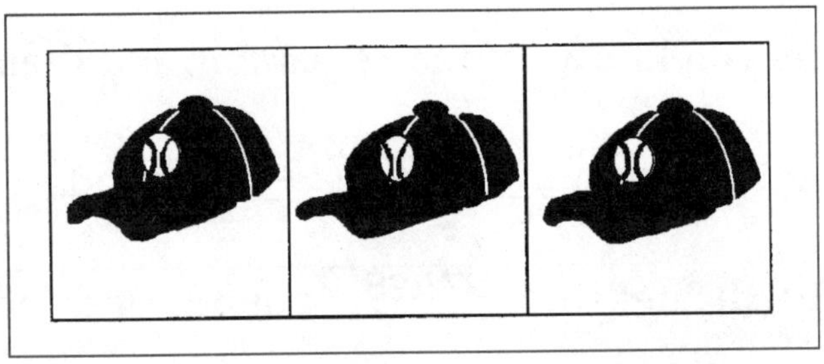

2. Elisa is on a community basketball team. She scores an average of 13.2 points a game. If there are 15 games in a season, about how many total points does she score in a season?

   a. Write a word equation that shows the problem's information.

   Average points per game = Total points **÷** Number of games

   b. For this problem, you can write an equivalent division equation for the Total points **in a season.**

   Number of games **x** Average points per game **= Total points**

   c. Write the numbers you know into the equation, and then solve.

   15 x 13.2 **=** 198 **points**

   So, Elisa scored a season total of about 198 **points.**

Name ______________________________

PRACTICE

For problems 3 and 4, write a word equation showing each problem's information. Then write an equivalent word equation for solving each problem, and solve.

3. Enrique buys 15 pounds of ground beef for a dinner party. He pays a total of $36.75 for the ground beef. **What is the cost per pound of the ground beef?**

   Total cost = Pounds of beef x Price per pound. Price per pound = Total cost ÷ Pounds of beef.

   36.75 ÷ 15 = 2.45.

   So, the cost per pound of ground beef is $ 2.45 **.**

4. Enrique also buys cheese pies to serve as dessert at his dinner party. **If he pays a total of $20.45, and he buys 5 cheese pies, what is the cost of each cheese pie?**

   Total cost = Cost per pie x Number of pies. Total cost ÷ Number of pies = Cost per pie.

   20.45 ÷ 5 = 4.09.

   So, the cost of each cheese pie is $ 4.09 **.**

Solve

5. It takes a machine in a factory 25.6 minutes to stamp 16 records. **How many minutes does it take the machine to stamp one record?**

   It takes the machine 1.6 minutes to stamp one record.

6. Jenny's favorite chicken lays an average of 3.6 eggs a week. **In a period of 15 weeks, about how many eggs will the chicken lay?**

   The chicken will lay about 54 eggs.

7. Jorge prints and sells his own photos. One day, he sells 4 equally priced photos for a total of $568.20. **How much does one photo cost?**

   One photo costs $142.05

8. Josh spends 2.8 hours a day talking on the phone. **In 21 days, how many hours does Josh spend talking on the phone?**

   In 21 days, Josh talks on the phone for 58.8 hours.

TEST-TAKING PRACTICE

Choose the best answer for each problem. In the answer section at the bottom of this page, fill in the box of your choice.

1. Margaret and Tim are planning their wedding dinner. They plan on 75 guests. The total cost for the dinner is $3,975. What is the cost for each guest?

   Which word equation would help you solve this problem? B

   A Total cost of dinner x Cost for each guest = 75
   B Total cost of dinner ÷ Number of guests = Cost for each guest
   C Total cost of dinner = Number of guests ÷ 75
   D Number of guests ÷ Total cost = Cost for each guest

2. **Jon and Ki invite 87 guests to their wedding. The cost for each guest is $12.67. What is the total cost of the wedding?** J

   J $1,102.29 L $2,897.51
   K $2,008.49 M $6,567.77

3. **Bryan and Sabina spent $750.00 for wedding flowers. The cost per flower was $2.00. How many flowers did they buy?** C

   A 3.75 C 375
   B 37.5 D 3,750

4. **Ed and Marcia invite 138 guests to their wedding. If the cost for each guest is $18.33, how much do they spend in total?** J

   J $2,529.54 L $4,284,94
   K $3,899.83 M $6,452.89

Write About It

Write an equation for the information in the problem. Then write an equivalent equation for solving the problem, and solve.

5. **Sharon and Jeremy go on a cruise for their honeymoon. The cruise costs $2,072.98 and lasts for 14 days. What is the cost of one day of the cruise?**

   Total cost of cruise = Cost of cruise per day x Number of days. Cost of cruise per day = Total cost of cruise ÷ Number of days.

   2,072.98 ÷ 14 = 148.07. So, one day of the cruise costs $148.07.

1. A ☐ B ☒ C ☐ D ☐
2. J ☒ K ☐ L ☐ M ☐
3. A ☐ B ☐ C ☒ D ☐
4. J ☒ K ☐ L ☐ M ☐

Name ______________________________

Organizing a List

Sometimes, you have to use a large amount of data to solve a problem. You can show the information in another way and organize it into a list.

Example

The table below lists the numbers of tickets sold for performances of a play. Find the mode and the median of ticket sales for the performances.

Tickets Sold for "The Trapped Mouse"

1/11	1/12	1/13	1/15	1/16	1/17	1/18	1/19	1/20	1/22	1/23	1/24	1/26	1/27	1/28
84	88	45	48	52	50	64	74	80	48	52	43	52	83	88

A. You'll find it helpful to list the ticket sales in order.

Step 1: First, find the least number. Read the table from left to right, and underline any number that you think may be the smallest one.

The first number I'll underline is 45.

Step 2: Keep reading. As you find other small numbers, compare each to the underlined number. Underline a new number if you need to.

I'll underline 43 and erase the line under 45.

Step 3: When you've finished reading the table, you'll have found the least number. Begin your list.

The least number in the list is 43. I'll cross it out in the table.

Step 4: Repeat the process to find the next smallest number in the table. Some numbers may appear more than once. Make sure you list each number as many times as it appears.

List the ticket sales in order from least to greatest.

43, 45, 48, 48, 50, 52, 52, 52, 64, 74, 80, 83, 84, 88, 88

B. Find the most frequent number in your organized list.

The number __52__ appears three times. **So, the mode is __52__.**

Find the middle number in your organized list.

The eighth number on the list is __52__. **So, the median is __52__.**

GUIDED PRACTICE

The table below lists the average monthly rainfall in Honolulu, Hawaii.

Honolulu's Average Monthly Rainfall, in Inches

Jan	Feb	Mar	Apr	May	Jun	Jul	Aug	Sep	Oct	Nov	Dec
3.6	2.2	2.2	1.5	1.1	0.5	0.6	0.4	0.8	2.3	3.0	3.8

1. What is the range of Honolulu's monthly rainfall?

   a. Write the information in order from least to greatest rainfall.

   0.4, 0.5, 0.6, 0.8, 1.1, 1.5, 2.2, 2.2, 2.3, 3.0, 3.6, 3.8

   b. What are the first and last numbers on your list? 0.4 **and** 3.8

   c. Find the difference between the numbers. 3.8 – 0.4 = 3.4

   So, the range is 3.4 **inches.**

2. Use the table to find the median high temperature during the week.

   a. Write the numbers in an ordered list.

   −5, −4, −2, −1, 1, 3, 5

   b. Find the middle number in the list.

   The fourth number is −1

   So, the median temperature is −1 **°C.**

Daily High Temperature

Sunday	−4°C
Monday	−5°C
Tuesday	−2°C
Wednesday	3°C
Thursday	5°C
Friday	−1°C
Saturday	1°C

3. Organizing data into a list can help you solve problems.

   a. How does organizing data help to find the range of a set of numbers?

   The first and last numbers are the ones you need.

   b. How does organizing data help to find the median of a set of numbers?

   It allows you to find the middle of the set.

Name ____________________

PRACTICE

The table below gives the high temperature recorded in Chicago, Illinois, on each day for one week.

Temperature in Chicago, Illinois

Day	High Temperature
Sunday	62°F
Monday	65°F
Tuesday	59°F
Wednesday	62°F
Thursday	67°F
Friday	70°F
Saturday	71°F

4. What is the order of temperatures from lowest to highest?

59°, 62°, 62°, 65°, 67°, 70°, 71°

5. On how many days was the temperature higher than 66°F?

3 days

6. What is the lowest temperature for the week?

59°F

7. On how many days was the high temperature lower than 70°F?

5 days

8. What is the highest temperature for the week?

71°F

9. What is the mode of the high temperatures for the week?

62°F

10. What is the range of the high temperatures for the week?

12 degrees

11. What is the median high temperature for the week?

65°F

TEST-TAKING PRACTICE

Use the table to choose the best answer for problems 1–6. In the answer section at the bottom of the page, fill in the box of your choice.

Daily Attendance at Reptile World

Sunday	Monday	Tuesday	Wednesday	Thursday	Friday	Saturday
88	43	52	55	52	67	83

1. Which set of numbers lists the attendance in order from least to greatest? B

A 43, 52, 55, 67, 83, 88
B 43, 52, 52, 55, 67, 83, 88
C 88, 83, 67, 55, 52, 52, 43
D 88, 43, 52, 55, 52, 67, 83, 88

2. On how many days did more than 70 people visit Reptile World? M

J 3 days
K 4 days
L 5 days
M 2 days

3. If attendance on Saturday increased by 2, what would happen to the range? D

A It would increase by 2.
B It would decrease by 2.
C It would double.
D It would stay the same.

4. What is the median of the daily attendance figures at Reptile World? L

J 43
K 52
L 55
M 88

5. How would you find the range of attendance at Reptile World? D

A Add the lowest number to the highest number.
B Add the lowest number to the highest, and divide by 2.
C Choose the middle number in the list.
D Subtract the lowest number from the highest number.

6. What is the mode of the daily attendance figures at Reptile World? K

J 43
K 52
L 55
M 88

Write About It

7. Why is it helpful to organize data into an ordered list to find the median of the data?

Students should explain that the median of a set of numbers is that number that is in the exact middle of an ordered list of the numbers.

1. A ☐ B ☒ C ☐ D ☐
2. J ☐ K ☐ L ☐ M ☒
3. A ☐ B ☐ C ☐ D ☒
4. J ☐ K ☐ L ☒ M ☐
5. A ☐ B ☐ C ☐ D ☒
6. J ☐ K ☒ L ☐ M ☐

Name ______________________________

Reading a Line Graph

The information that you need to solve a problem may be presented in a line graph. Line graphs are often used to show a change over time.

The graph at the right shows the daily high temperature for one week in January. The horizontal axis of a line graph usually shows time intervals. On this graph, the horizontal axis shows the date for each temperature reading. The vertical axis on the graph shows the high temperature reading for each day.

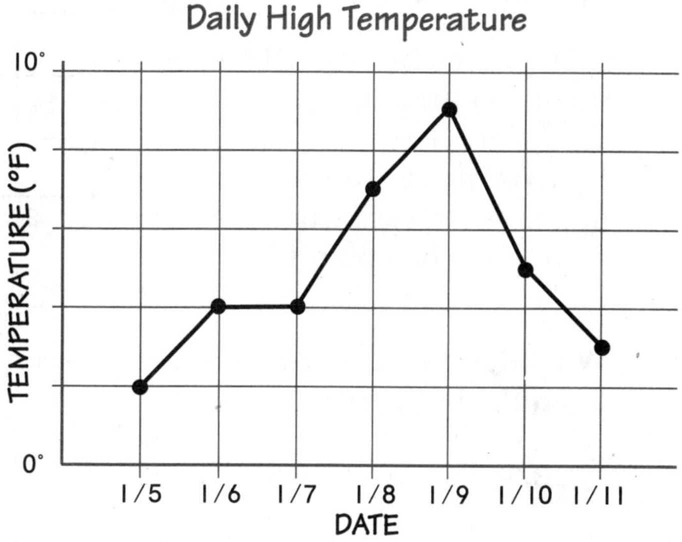

Example

What was the high temperature on January 10?

A. Find the value of each interval on the vertical axis. Use a finger to count the number of intervals between 0° and 10°.

Divide the range, which is 10°, by the number of intervals.

10 ÷ ___5___ = ___2___. So, each interval represents 2°.

B. Look for the point plotted directly above 1/10 on the horizontal axis. Run your finger along the grid lines from the point. Mark the corresponding place on the vertical axis with a pencil, and write in the value of the grid line. If the point is between two grid lines, mark the values of both.

Which values is the point halfway between?

___4°F and 6°F___

So, the high temperature was ___5°F___.

GUIDED PRACTICE

Use the line graph at the right to find the information you need to solve the problems.

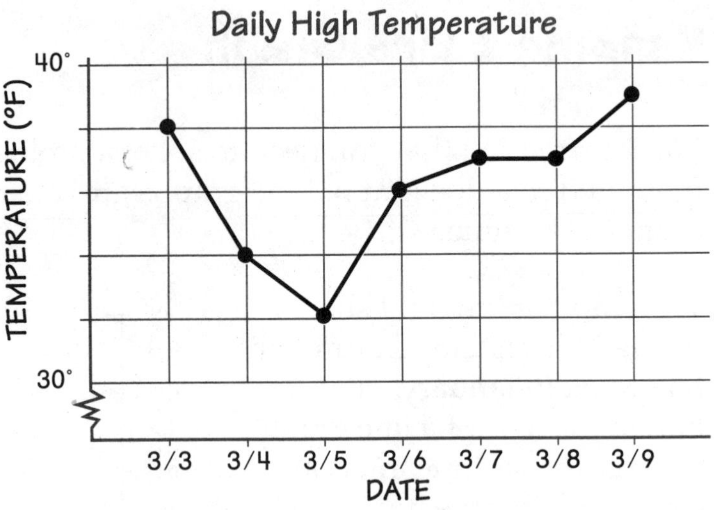

1. On which two days was the temperature the lowest?

   a. Look for the two lowest points on the graph—the points closest to the horizontal axis. Run your finger downward from each of the two points to the horizontal axis.

   What dates do the two points correspond to on the horizontal axis?

   3/4 and 3/5

   b. So, the temperature was lowest on

   March 4 **and** March 5.

> Notice that this graph has a break at the bottom—the temperatures begin at 30°F. The break lets you know that there are no readings between 0°F and 30°F.

2. How many degrees did the temperature change between March 5 and March 6?

   a. Find the value of the intervals on the vertical axis.

   How many degrees does each interval represent?

   2 degrees

   b. Look for points directly above 3/5 and 3/6 on the horizontal axis. Run your finger from those two points to the vertical axis.

   What values do the two points have on the vertical axis?

   32°F and 36°F

   c. Subtract to find the temperature change.

   What is the difference between the two readings?

   4 degrees

   So, the temperature changed 4 **degrees.**

Name ___________________________________

PRACTICE

Use the line graph to find the information you need to solve the problems.

The graph shows annual production of soybeans in the United States for the years 1985 through 1990. The production is given in bushels per acre.

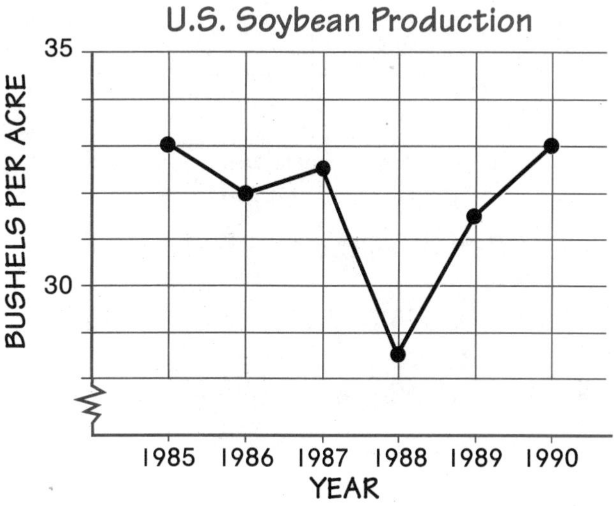

3. **How many bushels per acre of soybeans were produced in 1987?**

   32.5 bushels per acre

4. **In which year was soybean production the lowest?**

   1988

5. **In which two years was the production of soybeans the same?**

   1985 and 1990

6. **By how much did soybean production decrease between 1987 and 1988?**

   It decreased by 4 bushels per acre.

Solve

7. **In how many years was soybean production greater than 32 bushels per acre? Which years were they?**

   3 years; 1985, 1987, 1990

8. **Between which two years was there the greatest change in soybean production?**

   1987 and 1988

9. How many more bushels per acre were produced in 1990 than in 1988?

   There were 4.5 more bushels per acre produced in 1990.

10. **Between which two years was there the least change in soybean production? What was the change?**

    1986 and 1987; the change was an increase of 0.5 bushels per acre.

TEST-TAKING PRACTICE

Choose the best answer for each problem. In the answer section at the bottom of the page, fill in the box of your choice.

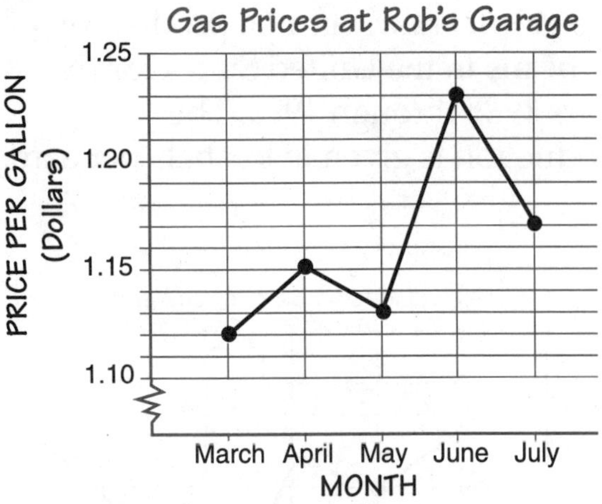

1. What does the graph show? C

A the average monthly price per liter of gasoline
B the average yearly price per liter of gasoline
C the average monthly price per gallon of gasoline
D the average yearly price per gallon of gasoline

2. What was the price per gallon of gasoline in July? M

J $1.13 L $1.23
K $1.16 M $1.17

3. Which choice correctly describes the change in gasoline prices from May to June? C

A an increase from $1.13 to $1.15
B a decrease from $1.23 to $1.19
C an increase from $1.13 to $1.23
D They remained the same.

4. If you had bought 10 gallons of gasoline at Rob's Garage in April, how much would you have paid? L

J $11.30 L $11.50
K $12.30 M $11.20

5. Which choice correctly describes the change in gasoline prices from March to April? A

A They increased by 3 cents.
B They decreased by 3 cents.
C They decreased by 2 cents.
D They remained the same.

6. What was the overall change in the price of a gallon of gasoline from March to July? K

J It dropped by 5 cents.
K It increased by 5 cents.
L It lasted for 4 months.
M Not given

Write About It

7. Explain why there is a break in the vertical axis of the graph between 0 and $1.10.

None of the average monthly prices for gasoline were less than $1.10.

1.	A ☐	B ☐	C ☒	D ☐	4.	J ☐	K ☐	L ☒	M ☐
2.	J ☐	K ☐	L ☐	M ☒	5.	A ☒	B ☐	C ☐	D ☐
3.	A ☐	B ☐	C ☒	D ☐	6.	J ☐	K ☒	L ☐	M ☐

Name ____________________

Interpreting Changes in a Line Graph

The direction and steepness of the lines connecting the points in a line graph can provide the information you need to solve a problem.

- A horizontal line shows no change.
- A line sloping upward shows an increase.
- A line sloping downward shows a decrease.

Carla's Savings at the Beginning of Each Month

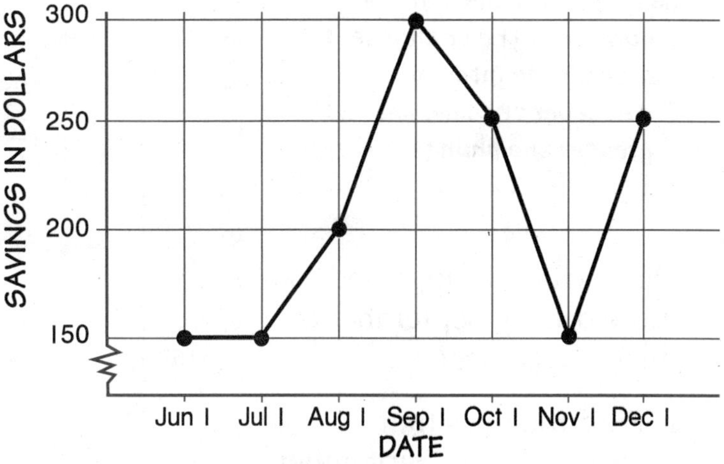

So, the line sloping upward between November 1 and December 1 shows that Carla's savings increased during November.

Example 1

In which months did Carla's savings decrease?

A. Look for lines in the graph that slope downward.

B. Find the months on the horizontal axis that correspond to those lines.

In which months does the line slope downward?

September **and** October

So, Carla's savings decreased in September **and** October.

Example 2

In which month did Carla's savings stay the same?

Step 1: Look for a line in the graph that has no slope.

Step 2: Find the month on the horizontal axis that corresponds to that line. In which month is the line horizontal?

June

So, Carla's savings stayed the same in June.

GUIDED PRACTICE

Use the line graph of Carla's savings to find the information you need to solve the problems.

> The slope of a line can tell you how great the change is over a time interval. The steeper the line, the greater the change.

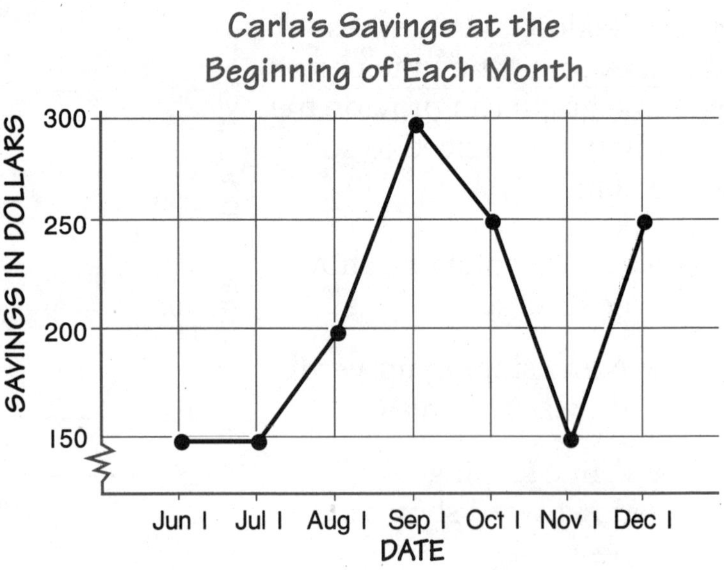

1. Did Carla's savings decrease more during September or during October?

   a. Find the lines that correspond to September and October. Compare the slopes of the two lines.

   Which of the two lines has the steeper downward slope?

   the line for October

   b. So, Carla's savings decreased more during October.

2. During which months did Carla's savings increase by the same amount?

   a. Find the lines in the graph that slope upward. Compare the steepness of the slopes of those lines.

   Which lines slope upward with the same steepness?

   the lines for August **and** November

   b. So, Carla's savings increased by the same amount during August **and** November.

3. Did Carla save more during July or August?

   a. Find the lines that correspond to July and August. Compare the slope of the two lines.

   Which of the two lines has the steeper upward slope?

   the line for August

   b. So, Carla saved more during August.

Name ______________________________ **Chapter 4** **L3**

PRACTICE

Use the line graph to find the information you need to solve the problems.

The graph shows the population of Juniper Island over a five-year period.

4. **Between which two dates did the population of Juniper Island stay the same?**

   1/1/1995 and 1/1/1996

5. **Did the population of Juniper Island increase or decrease during 1996?**

   It increased.

6. **During which year did the population of Juniper Island decrease?**

   1997

Population of Juniper Island, 1994–1999

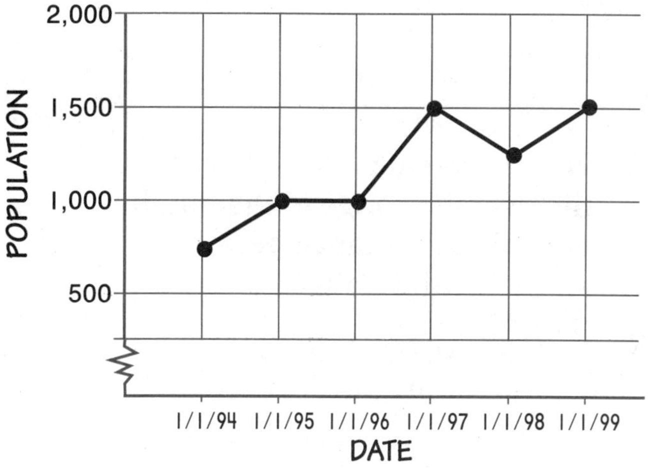

Solve

To solve these problems you may mark or draw on the graph.

7. **Did the population increase more during 1994 or during 1996?**

   during 1996

8. **During which two years was the increase in the population the same?**

   1994 and 1998

9. **During which year was there the greatest increase in the population of Juniper Island?**

   during 1996

10. **Did the population of Juniper Island increase, decrease, or stay the same for the period shown on the graph?**

    The population increased.

TEST-TAKING PRACTICE

Use the graph to choose the best answer for each problem. In the answer section at the bottom of the page, fill in the box of your choice.

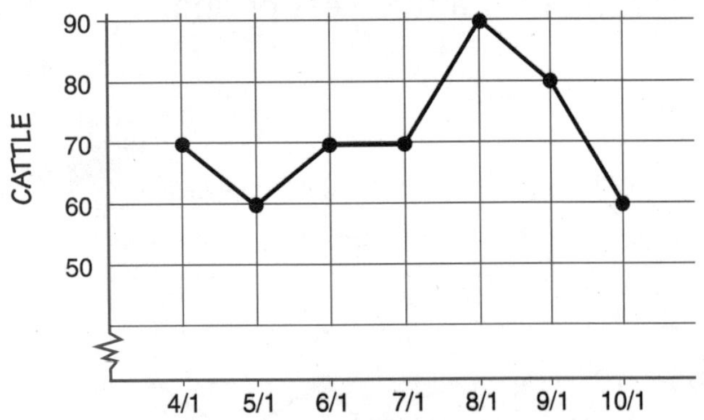

1. Which statement best describes the overall change in the number of cattle at the ranch between April 1 and October 1? B

A The number increased.
B The number decreased.
C The number stayed the same.
D You can't tell from the graph.

2. How did the number of cattle change during June? M

J It increased.
K It decreased.
L 70 cows
M It stayed the same.

3. Which months show the same decrease in the number of cattle? A

A April and August
B April and September
C May and July
D May and June

4. When did the greatest decrease in the number of cattle over one month take place? L

J during August
K during April
L during September
M during July

5. Which statement best describes the change in the number of cattle between April 1 and June 1? D

A It stayed the same and then dropped.
B It dropped and then stayed the same.
C It increased and then dropped.
D It dropped and then increased.

Write About It

6. Can you use the graph to find out how many cattle there were at the ranch in the middle of each month? Explain.

No. The plotted points show only the number of cattle on the first of each month.

1. A ☐ B ☒ C ☐ D ☐
2. J ☐ K ☐ L ☐ M ☒
3. A ☒ B ☐ C ☐ D ☐
4. J ☐ K ☐ L ☒ M ☐
5. A ☐ B ☐ C ☐ D ☒

Name ______________________________

Finding Data in a News Article

Sometimes, the information required to solve a problem is in a newspaper article. You can underline information that you need.

Page 1

Burton Computers Announces Record Sales Month

by Thom Barrett

Burton City, December 10 – Burton Computers, Burton City's leading computer software store, is a very busy place these days. Lois Halbert, the store manager, calls last month's sales "the best ever."

"In November, we sold 60 copies of *Astro Rider*, 45 copies of *Ocean Adventure*, and 27 copies of *Math Wizard*," said Halbert. "Of course, November is usually a good month for sales. But this was the best ever," she added.

The popular *Math Wizard* educational software sells for $12.50, while the *Astro Rider* and *Ocean Adventure* games each sell for $8.75.

Burton Computers also introduced the new software package *Hills and Thrills* in late November. "We sold 21 copies of *Hills and Thrills* the first week it was out," said Halbert. "We expect it to be our leading software seller by early next year."

Continued on Page 2

Example

How much money did Burton Computers take in from November sales of *Ocean Adventure*?

Step 1: Read the problem carefully.

What information do you need to solve the problem?

the ___number___ of copies of *Ocean Adventure* sold, and the ___price___ of each copy

Step 2: Reread the article. Underline the information you need as you read.

How many copies of *Ocean Adventure* were sold? ___45___

What is the price of each copy of *Ocean Adventure*? ___$8.75___

Step 3: Multiply to solve the problem.

What is the product of the number of sales and the price?

___45___ x ___8.75___ = ___393.75___

So, Burton Computers took in $ ___393.75___ from November sales of *Ocean Adventure*.

GUIDED PRACTICE

Use the continuation of the article, below, to answer the questions.

continued from page 1

"Of course, *Astro Rider* has been our best-selling software package for the last year," explained Ms. Halbert. "We are very pleased about that, because it's fun and educational. The game teaches a lot of fun things about space." Ms. Halbert went on to say that July sales of *Astro Rider* amounted to 22 copies; August and September sales totaled 47 copies each month; 39 copies were sold in October, and 60 copies in November. "That's a great sales record in any store," said Ms. Halbert.

1. How many more copies of *Astro Rider* were sold in August than in July?

Step 1: Read the problem.

What information do you need to solve the problem?

the number of copies sold in

__August__ and in __July__.

Step 2: Reread the article, underlining the needed information.

How many copies were sold in August?

__47__

How many copies were sold in July?

__22__

Step 3: Subtract to solve the problem.

__47__ – __22__ = __25__

So, __25__ more copies were sold in August than in July.

For problem 2, use another color to underline needed information.

2. How many copies of *Astro Rider* were sold from July through November?

Step 1: Read the problem.

What information do you need to solve the problem?

the __number of copies__ sold for each of the 5 months

Step 2: Reread the article, underlining the needed information.

How many copies were sold?

__22__, __47__, __47__, __39__, __60__

Step 3: Add to solve the problem.

__22__ + __47__ + __47__ + __39__

+ __60__ = __22__

So, __215__ copies were sold from July through November.

Name ______________________________

PRACTICE

Use this article to find the needed information to solve problems 3–6.

Seeing Things in a Different Light

You can tell it's winter—it's already dark when you get home from work. And the welcoming porch light has burned out again. It seems you changed that hard-to-reach lightbulb just last week. Lightbulbs don't last very long. However, scientists have recently come up with a bright idea.

The E-bulb is a new lightbulb that works by making radio waves! Yes, it's a mystery to me, too, but it really works. Scientists say that an E-bulb should last for about 14 years. A regular bulb usually lasts less than a single year. E-bulbs will also use much less electricity. A regular bulb lit for 24 hours a day costs about $1.50 a week to power. An E-bulb would cost only about $0.45. Less electricity means less burning of fossil fuels and less pollution from power plants, as well as less to pay when the electric bill arrives.

So what's the drawback? Well, an E-bulb will probably sell for about $15—that's 20 times as much as a regular bulb. But because of its long life and low running costs, it will still save you money as it welcomes you home on those dark winter nights.

3. What information do you need to find out how much it would cost to light an E-bulb all the time for 52 weeks—a whole year? How much would it cost?

how much it costs to run it for one week;
52 x $0.45 = $23.40. It would cost
$23.40 to light an E-bulb for one year.

4. What information in the news article can you use to find out how much a regular lightbulb sells for? How much does a regular bulb sell for?

An E-bulb costs $15. It costs 20 times as
much as a regular bulb. $15 ÷ 20 = $0.75.
A regular bulb sells for $0.75.

Solve . . . .

5. About how much does it cost to keep a regular bulb lit all day?

It costs about $0.21.

6. How much longer than a regular bulb should an E-bulb last?

It should last about 13 years longer.

TEST-TAKING PRACTICE

Use this article to help you choose the best answer for each problem.

A Walk in the Park

They have been walking for 4 days now and have covered 50 miles of trails through Canyonlands National Park in Utah. Most of the group of hikers have blisters, and a few have sunburned faces and arms. But nobody is ready to call it a day. As one hiker says, "Joe wouldn't quit, and neither will I."

She's referring to Joe Hendrix, a retired schoolteacher from Arizona, who founded "A Walk in the Park" in 1994. In the years since, a total of 625 people—students, professionals, and even a handful of celebrities—have taken time from their busy schedules to walk the trails of America's national parks. Each hiker pays $55 for the privilege of roughing it for a week. It's another $80 for the specialized equipment that the hiker will use. Food for the outing costs $65. (Clean socks are each hiker's own responsibility.) Groups of volunteers travel through the national parks, making measurements, taking readings, and comparing data. The information that they gather is used by Joe's organization in its studies of the environment.

1. **Which equation shows the amount each hiker pays?** B

   A $80 + $65 = $145
   B $55 + $80 + $65 = $200
   C $55 + $80 = $135
   D Not given

2. **Which information would you use to find the average distance the hikers covered each day?** L

   J Each hiker pays $55 for the privilege of roughing it for a week.
   K A total of 625 people have taken time.
   L They have walked for 4 days and have covered 50 miles.
   M Joe Hendrix founded "A Walk in the Park" in 1994.

3. **If each group includes 25 people, how many groups have taken "A Walk in the Park?"** A

   A 25 C 625
   B 50 M 1994

Write About It

Write a plan, and then solve.

4. **If the group plans to hike 84 miles, how would you find how many more miles they must travel?**

   Read the article to find how far the group has traveled (50 miles), and subtract that distance from 84 miles. 84 – 50 = 34. They must travel 34 more miles.

1. A ❑ B ☒ C ❑ D ❑
2. J ❑ K ❑ L ☒ M ❑
3. A ☒ B ❑ C ❑ D ❑

Reading a Circle Graph

Sometimes, you will find the information you need to solve a problem in a circle graph. A circle graph compares the parts of a whole.

The youth club held a walk-a-thon to raise funds for the youth center. The graph shows how the raised funds were used.

A. The title of the circle graph describes what the whole circle represents. The sectors of the circle show the parts that make up the whole. The size of each sector shows you how large a portion of the whole it represents.

B. You can compare two sectors by comparing their central angles.

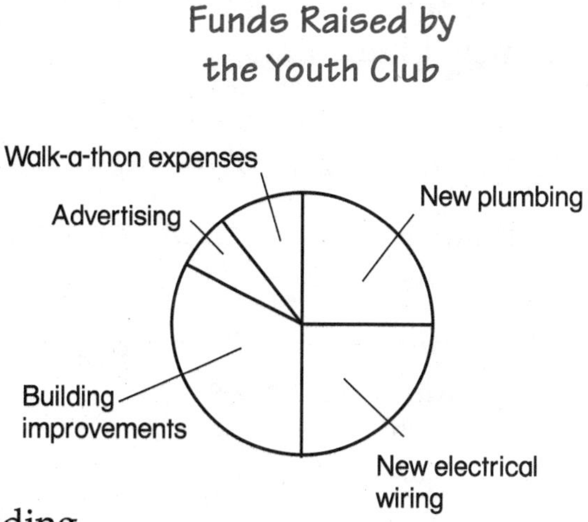

Example 1

Did the club use more of the funds for building improvements or for new plumbing for the youth center?

Step 1: Find the sectors labeled "building improvements" and "new plumbing."

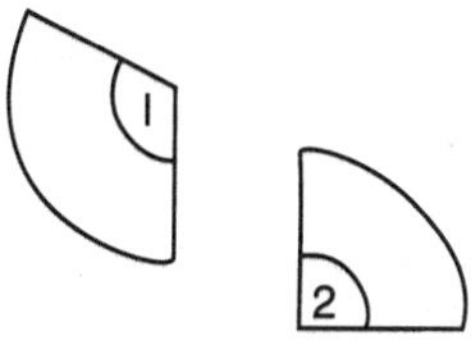

Step 2: Compare the size of the two sectors.
Which of the two sectors is larger?

Angle 1 is greater than 90°, and angle 2 is 90°.

The sector labeled ___building improvements___ is larger.

So, the club used more funds for ___building improvements___.

C. You can use the size of the central angle to estimate the fraction of the whole that a sector shows.

Example 2

About what fraction of the funds raised was used for new electrical wiring for the youth center?

Step 1: Find the sector labeled "new electrical wiring."

Step 2: Compare the size of the two sectors.

About how much of the circle is taken up by that sector? ___about one-fourth___

So, about ___about one-fourth___ **of the funds was used for new wiring.**

GUIDED PRACTICE

Use the circle graph of the youth club's funds to find the information you need to solve the problems.

Notice that the title of the graph now tells you that the whole circle represents $1,000.

Funds Raised by the Youth Club – $1,000

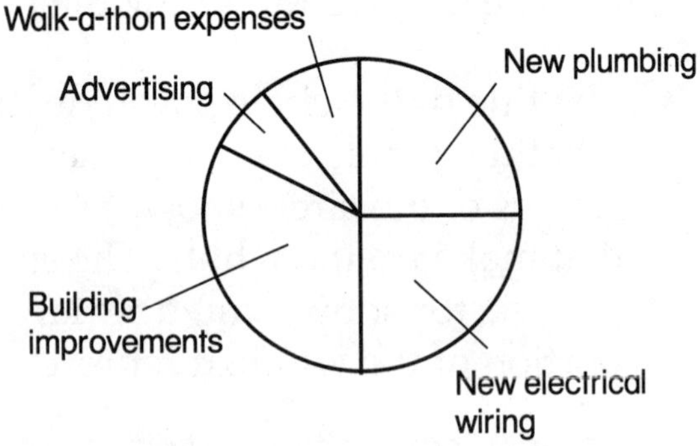

1. About how much did the club spend for new plumbing?

   a. Find the sector labeled "new plumbing."

   Estimate what fraction of the circle it represents.

   About how much of the circle is taken up by the plumbing sector?

   about one-fourth

   b. Multiply the whole amount, $1,000, by the fraction.

   $1000 x $\frac{1}{4}$ = $ 250

   So, the club spent about 250 on new plumbing.

2. Which project did the club spend about $300 on?

   a. Find what fraction $300 is of $1,000. 300 ÷ 1,000 = $\frac{3}{10}$

   b. Find that sector on the graph that is about $\frac{3}{10}$ of the whole.

   Which sector takes up about $\frac{3}{10}$ of the circle?

   (*Hint*: $\frac{3}{10}$ is greater than one fourth.)

   The sector labeled building improvements takes up about $\frac{3}{10}$ of the circle.

   So, the club spent about $300 on building improvements.

3. Did the club spend more on plumbing or on advertising and expenses?

   a. Find the sectors with the corresponding labels. Compare the size of the plumbing sector with the *combined* size of the advertising and expenses sectors.

   Which takes up more of the circle? plumbing

   b. So, the club spent more on plumbing.

Name ____________________

PRACTICE

Use the circle graph to find the information you need to solve the problems.

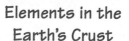

The circle graph shows the elements in the earth's crust.

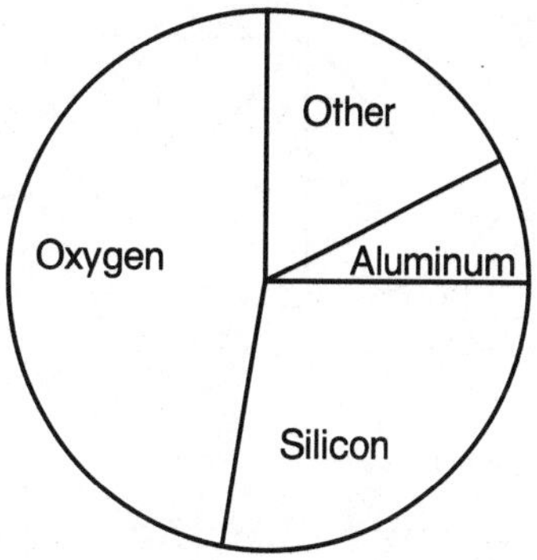

4. **What are the three most common elements in the earth's crust?**

   oxygen, silicon, and aluminum

5. **What is the most common element in the earth's crust?**

   oxygen

6. **About how much of the earth's crust is made up of silicon?**

   about one-fourth

Solve

To solve these problems, you might find it helpful to mark or draw on the graph.

7. **Does oxygen make up more than half of the earth's crust or less than half of the earth's crust?**

   less than half

8. **Do aluminum and silicon together make up more or less of the earth's crust than oxygen?**

   less

9. **About how many tons of silicon would there be in a representative sample of 10 tons of the earth's crust?**

   Accept answers between 2.5 and 3 tons.

10. **Which element would make up nearly 1 ton of a representative sample of 10 tons of the earth's crust?**

    aluminum

TEST-TAKING PRACTICE

Use the graph to choose the best answer for problems 1–6. In the answer section at the bottom of the page, fill in the box of your choice.

A Collection of 80
Animal Trading Cards

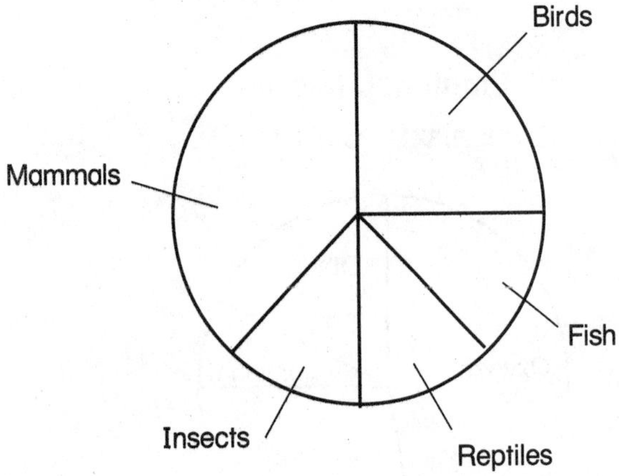

1. **Which of the following cards make up the same fraction of the total amount of cards as the mammal trading cards?** D

   A fish and reptile cards together
   B insect and reptile cards together
   C fish and insect cards together
   D bird and fish cards together

2. **About what fraction of the collection do fish cards account for?** K

   J $\frac{1}{10}$ **L** $\frac{1}{6}$
   K $\frac{1}{8}$ **M** $\frac{1}{4}$

3. **Which cards account for one-fourth of the collection?** A

   A Birds   **C** Insects
   B Fish   **D** Mammals

4. **How would you compare reptile and insect cards?** L

   J There are more insect cards.
   K There are more reptile cards.
   L There are the same number of each.
   M There are twice as many insect cards.

5. **About how many bird cards are there in the collection?** B

   A 10   **C** 30
   B 20   **D** 40

6. **Which group has at least 10 cards?** L

   J Fish   **L** Every group
   K Reptiles   **M** Not given

Write About It

7. **Why is a circle graph a useful way of showing how the parts of a whole compare?**

   Students should point out that a circle graph lets you compare each sector to the whole and to each other sector.

1.	A ☐	B ☐	C ☐	D ☒
2.	J ☐	K ☒	L ☐	M ☐
3.	A ☒	B ☐	C ☐	D ☐
4.	J ☐	K ☐	L ☒	M ☐
5.	A ☐	B ☒	C ☐	D ☐
6.	J ☐	K ☐	L ☒	M ☐

Name ______________________

Reading a Double-Bar Graph

A double-bar graph compares related sets of information. The graph below compares the numbers of viewers of the season premieres in 1998 and 1999 for four television shows.

Example

How many more viewers did *The Thompsons* have in 1999 than in 1998?

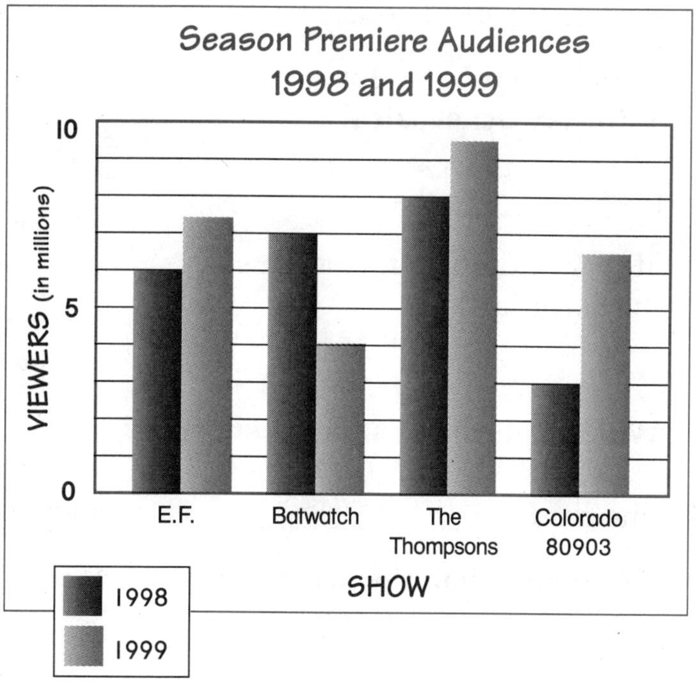

A. Find the double bar that is labeled *The Thompsons*.

B. The **key** next to the graph tells you what each bar represents.

The black bar shows the number of viewers in 1998.

The red bar shows the number of viewers in ___1999___.

C. Find the value of each interval on the vertical axis.

Count the number of intervals between 0 and 5 million.

There are ___5___ intervals.

So, each interval represents ___1 million or 1,000,000___ **viewers.**

D. Now find the number of viewers of *The Thompsons* in each year. If the value lies between grid lines, estimate the amount.

***The Thompsons* had** ___8 million or 8,000,000___ **viewers in 1998.**

***The Thompsons* had** ___about 9.5 million or 9,500,000___ **viewers in 1999.**

E. Subtract to solve.

9.5 – ___8___ = ___1.5___

So, *The Thompsons* had ___about 1.5 million or 1,500,000___ **more viewers in 1999 than in 1998.**

GUIDED PRACTICE

Use the double-bar graph to answer the questions.

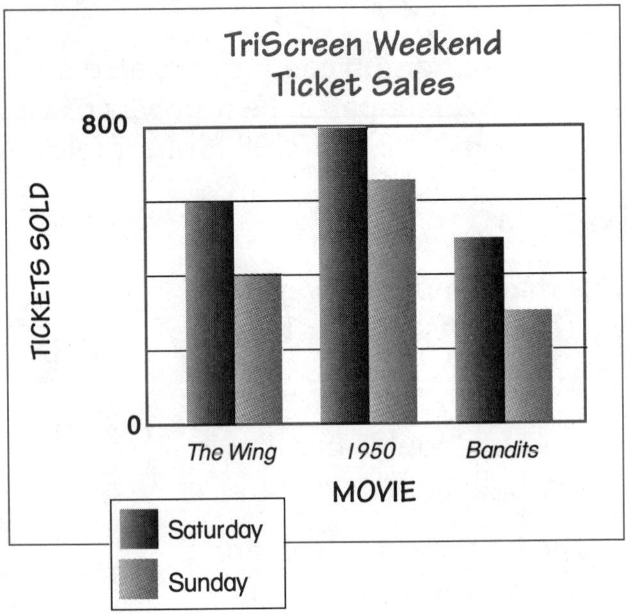

1. Which of the three movies had the lowest ticket sales on Saturday?

   Step 1: Find the bars that represent Saturday ticket sales.

   Which color bars represent Saturday ticket sales?

   the black bars

   Step 2: Compare the heights of the Saturday bars.

   Which Saturday bar is the shortest?

   The bar for Bandits is the shortest.

   So, *Bandits* had the lowest ticket sales on Saturday.

2. Which movie had ticket sales of 650 tickets? On which day?

   Step 1: Find the value of each interval on the vertical axis.

   How many intervals are there between 0 and 800? 4

   Divide 800 by the number of intervals. 800 ÷ 4 = 200

   So, each interval represents 200 tickets sold.

   Step 2: Find the bar that corresponds to a value of about 650 on the vertical axis.

   THINK: The value 650 will be between 600 and 800, but it will be closer to 600.

   Which bar corresponds to about 650?

   the red bar for the movie 1950

   So, 1950 **had ticket sales of about 650 on** Sunday.

Name ______________________

PRACTICE

Use the double-bar graph to answer the questions.

3. Which vendor sold the most hot dogs?

Harrison

4. Which vendor sold the most pretzels?

Vinnie

5. Which vendor sold 30 pretzels?

Harrison

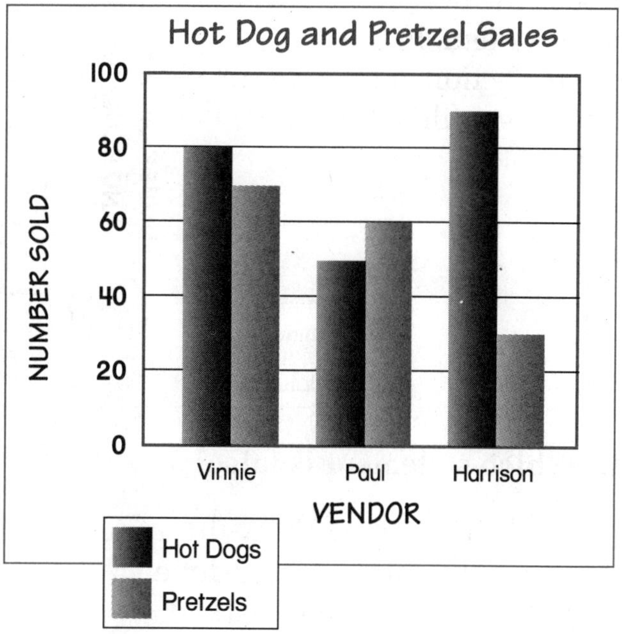

Solve

6. How many more hot dogs did Harrison sell than Paul sold?

Harrison sold 40 more hot dogs.

7. How many more hot dogs than pretzels did Harrison sell?

Harrison sold 60 more hot dogs.

8. How many hot dogs and pretzels did Paul sell all together?

Paul sold 110 items all together.

9. Which of the three vendors sold 10 more pretzels than hot dogs?

Paul sold 10 more pretzels.

10. Hot dogs and pretzels each sell for the same amount. Which of the three vendors took in the most money from sales?

Vinnie took in the most money.

11. If hot dogs and pretzels sell for the same amount, did the vendors take in more money from selling hot dogs or from selling pretzels?

The vendors took in more money from selling hot dogs.

TEST-TAKING PRACTICE

Use the double-bar graph to answer the questions. Choose the best answer for each problem. In the answer section at the bottom of the page, fill in the box of your choice.

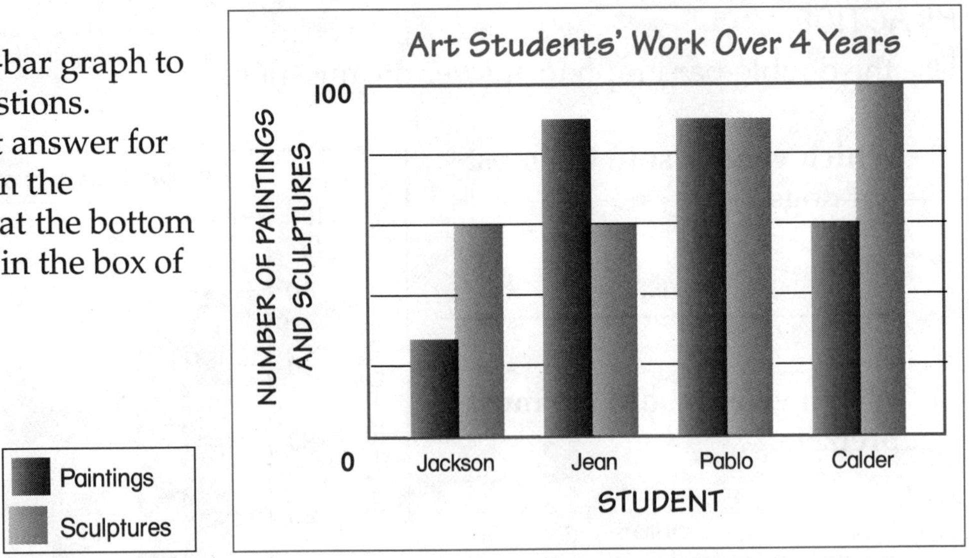

1. **Which statement is false?** D

   A The black bars show the number of paintings done.
   B Jackson and Jean made the same number of sculptures.
   C Pablo made the same number of paintings and sculptures.
   D Calder made the most paintings.

2. **Which statement is true?** K

   J The gray bars show the number of paintings done.
   K Pablo made the same number of paintings as Jean.
   L Calder made the most paintings.
   M Jackson made 60 paintings.

3. **Which art student made the most sculptures?** D

   A Jackson **C** Pablo
   B Jean **D** Calder

4. **How many paintings did the four students make combined?** L

   J 100 **L** 270
   K 250 **M** 310

5. **How many works did Jackson make in all?** A

   A 90 **C** 60
   B 150 **D** 30

Write About It

6. **If each student also made a number of photographs, how could you show the data in the graph?**

   You could show this information in the graph by adding a different-color bar next to the existing bars.

1. A ☐ B ☐ C ☐ D ☒
2. J ☐ K ☒ L ☐ M ☐
3. A ☐ B ☐ C ☐ D ☒
4. J ☐ K ☐ L ☒ M ☐
5. A ☒ B ☐ C ☐ D ☐

Name ____________________

Test-Taking Skill: Eliminating Choices

On a multiple choice test, it's sometimes hard to find the right answer to a problem. It can help to eliminate choices that are wrong.

Example

Karen is ordering buttons for the bike club. The buttons cost \$0.13 each if she buys 100 and \$0.11 each if she buys more than 300. She decides to buy 750 buttons. How much will she pay?

A \$11.00 **C** \$97.50
B \$82.50 **D** 300

Step 1: Read the problem carefully. Think about the kind of answer you need. The answer to "How much will she pay?" is an amount of money. So, choice **D** must be wrong.

Step 2: Karen will pay \$0.11 per button because she is buying more than 300 buttons. Estimate to eliminate choices.

THINK: The price of \$0.11 is close to \$0.10, and 750 x \$0.10 is \$75.00.

\$0.11 is more than \$0.10, which tells you that the answer has to be more than \$75.00. So, choice **A**, \$11.00, is too small.

You can eliminate choice **A**.

The choices left are choice **B**, \$82.50, and choice **C**, \$97.50.

Both are greater than \$75.00.

Divide or multiply to find the correct answer:

B → \$82.50 ÷ 0.11 = \$750 750 x \$0.11= \$82.50

Karen will pay \$82.50 for 750 buttons.

So, the correct answer is B.

TEST-TAKING PRACTICE

Choose the best answer for each problem. In the answer section at the bottom of this page, fill in the box of your choice. For problem 1, explain how you found the answer.

1. The marching band sold T-shirts for $7.50 each. They sold 36 T-shirts at the game.

How much money did they earn? C

A 270 T-shirts C $270.00
B $27.00 D $2,700

Choice A is the wrong kind of answer. Choice B is too small an amount, because 10 shirts would sell for $75. Choice D is too great an amount, because 100 shirts would sell for $750.00. The correct choice is choice C.

2. The sign at the Super Cinema has 15 rows of lightbulbs. Each row has 220 bulbs.

How many bulbs are there in all? M

J 220 bulbs L 330 bulbs
K 220 rows M 3,300 bulbs

3. A jet airplane flies at about 580 miles per hour.

About how many miles can it travel in 4 hours? B

A About 200 miles per hour
B About 2,400 miles
C About 5,800 miles
D About 7,400 miles

4. A housefly lays 120 eggs. Half of the eggs hatch and become female flies.

If each of those females lays 120 eggs, how many flies would hatch in the next generation? M

J 60 eggs L 720 flies
K 120 flies M 7,200 flies

5. The speed at which Pluto orbits the sun is 2.9 miles per second. Mercury orbits the sun 10 times as fast as Pluto.

How fast does Mercury move? C

A 10 miles per second
B 29 miles an hour
C 29 miles per second
D 290 miles per second

1. A ☐ B ☐ C ☒ D ☐
2. J ☐ K ☐ L ☐ M ☒
3. A ☐ B ☒ C ☐ D ☐
4. J ☐ K ☐ L ☐ M ☒
5. A ☐ B ☐ C ☒ D ☐

Name ______________________________

Using a Table to Rename Measures

To solve some measurement problems, you'll have to rename a measure with a different unit. If you don't already know the equivalent measures, you can find the needed information in a table like the one below.

Metric Units of Measure

Units of Length	Units of Capacity	Units of Mass
1 meter (m) = 1,000 millimeters (mm)	1 kiloliter (kL) = 1,000 liters (L)	1 gram (g) = 1,000 milligrams (mg)
1 meter (m) = 100 centimeters (cm)	1 liter = 1,000 milliliters (mL)	1 kilogram (kg) = 1,000 grams (g)
1 kilometer (km) = 1,000 meters		

Example

There is a 2-kg bag of iron filings and a 200-g bag of calcium carbonate in the cupboard. Drew's science teacher asks him to bring the heavier bag. Which bag should Drew bring?

A. Look at the problem carefully.

What measurements do you need to compare?

2 kg and 200 g

B. Look at the table. Find the column that shows grams and kilograms. Underline the equation that you need to use.

Write an equation to show how the units compare.

1 kg = 1,000 g

C. Rename the larger unit so that you can compare the measures. Multiply to get the measure that you need (2 kilograms).

2 kg = 2 x 1,000 g **2 kg = 2,000 g**

D. Now compare the two sizes of bags.

2,000 g > 200 g

2 kg is greater than 200 g.

So, Drew should bring the 2-kg bag.

GUIDED PRACTICE

Metric Units of Measure

Units of Length	Units of Capacity	Units of Mass
1 meter (m) = 1,000 millimeters (mm)	1 kiloliter (kL) = 1,000 liters (L)	1 gram (g) = 1,000 milligrams (mg)
1 meter = 100 centimeters (cm)	1 liter = 1,000 milliliters (mL)	1 kilogram (kg) = 1,000 grams
1 kilometer (km) = 1,000 meters		

1. Two bottles are filled with water. One bottle holds 750 mL and the other holds 0.6 L. Which bottle is smaller?

   a. What measurements do you need to compare? 750 mL and 0.6 L

   b. Find the appropriate column of the table.
   Write an equation for comparing the units.

   1 L = 1,000 mL

   c. Rename the larger measure by multiplying.

   0.6 L = 0.6 x 1,000 mL = 600 mL

   d. Compare the capacities of the bottles.

   600 mL < 750 mL

   So, the bottle holding 0.6 L **is the smaller bottle.**

2. Rolls of fabric come in two different widths: 120 cm and 1.75 m. Which is the wider roll?

   a. What measurements do you need to compare? 120 cm and 1.75 m

   b. Find the appropriate column of the table.
   Write an equation for comparing the units.

   1 m = 100 **cm**

   c. Rename the larger measure by multiplying.

   1.75 m = 1.75 **x 100 cm**

   d. Compare the widths of the rolls.

   175 **cm >** 120 **cm**

   So, the roll that is 1.75 m **wide is the wider roll.**

Name ______________________________ **Chapter 5 L1**

PRACTICE

Solve each problem by renaming one of the measures. If you wish, use the table below to find equivalent measures. Solutions may vary. Sample solutions are given.

Metric Units of Measure

Units of Length	Units of Capacity	Units of Mass
1 meter (m) = 1,000 millimeters (mm)	1 kiloliter (kL) = 1,000 liters (L)	1 gram (g) = 1,000 milligrams (mg)
1 meter = 100 centimeters (cm)	1 liter = 1,000 milliliters (mL)	1 kilogram (kg) = 1,000 grams
1 kilometer (km) = 1,000 meters		

3. The minimum requirement for a vitamin is 4 mg. A serving of cereal has 0.0033 g of the vitamin. **Would one serving be enough?**

   0.0033 x 1,000 = 3.3; 3.3 < 4

   One serving would not be enough.

4. Karin is mailing two packages. One has a mass of 3,500 g. The other has a mass of 1.8 kg. **Which package has the greater mass?**

   1.8 x 1,000 = 1,800; 1,800 < 3,500;

   the 3,500-g package.

5. Torkil runs 16 kilometers per week. Chris runs 10,000 meters per week? **Who runs farther?**

   16 x 1,000 = 16,000;

   16,000 > 10,000. Torkil runs farther.

6. A model car is 0.15 meter long and a model bus is 110 millimeters long. **Which model is longer?**

   0.15 x 1,000 = 150; 150 > 110.

   The model car is longer.

7. A 3-kg weight is on the left side of a balance scale. A 4,000-g weight is on the right side. **Which side is heavier?**

   The right side is heavier.

8. Katy can jump 120 cm high on Earth and 7 m high on the moon. **Which jump is higher?**

   The 7-m jump is higher.

9. One drinking glass holds 450 mL while another holds 0.5 L. **Which glass holds more?**

   The 0.5-L glass holds more.

10. A jar holds 1,850 mL of water. **If the water is poured into a 2-L saucepan, will the saucepan overflow?**

    The saucepan will not overflow.

TEST-TAKING PRACTICE

For problems 1–3, choose the best way to rename units for the problem. For problems 4 and 5, choose the best answer to fill in the blank. Use the table on page 87 if you need help with equivalents. In the answer section at the bottom of the page, fill in the box of your choice.

1. Jill is 154 cm tall, and Jim is 1.3 m tall. Who is taller? B

A 1.3 x 1,000 = 1,300 mm
B 1.3 x 100 = 130 cm
C 54 ÷ 10 = 5.4 m
D 0.3 x 1,000 = 300 mm

2. A beaker contains 1,500 mL of water. If the water is poured into a 2-L bowl, will it overflow? M

J 1,500 ÷ 2 = 750 mL
K 1,500 ÷ 100 = 15 L
L 2 x 100 = 200 mL
M 2 x 1,000 = 2,000 mL

3. A geologist discovered a fossil with a mass of 3.4 kg and another fossil with a mass of 1,670 g. Which fossil has the greater mass? C

A 1,670 x 1,000 = 1,670,000 mg
B 3.4 x 100 = 340 g
C 3.4 x 1,000 = 3,400 g
D 1,670 ÷ 100 = 16.7 kg

4. A 0.4-km race is ____ a 400-m race. J

J the same length as
K shorter than
L longer than
M twice as long as

5. A 2.2-kg box of nails has ____ a box of nails with a mass of 275 g. D

A the same mass as
B almost the same mass as
C less mass than
D greater mass than

Write About It

6. Which is the more reasonable estimate for the capacity of a bathtub: 20 L or 20 kL?

Write a plan for solving the problem. Then solve.

Sample answer: Rename 20 kL as liters. 20 x 1,000 = 20,000 L. So, 20,000 L is not reasonable; 20 L is the more reasonable estimate.

1. A ☐ B ☒ C ☐ D ☐
2. J ☐ K ☐ L ☐ M ☒
3. A ☐ B ☐ C ☒ D ☐
4. J ☒ K ☐ L ☐ M ☐
5. A ☐ B ☐ C ☐ D ☒

Name ______________________________________

Deciding How to Rename Customary Measures

When a problem has different units, you'll need to show the information in another way to solve the problem. When you rename measures, you multiply or divide. Drawing a picture can help you decide which to do.

Customary Units of Measure

Units of Length	Units of Capacity	Units of Mass
1 foot (ft) = 12 inches (in.)	1 cup (c) = 8 fluid ounces (fl oz)	1 pound (lb) = 16 ounces (oz)
1 yard (yd) = 3 feet	1 quart (qt) = 4 cups	1 ton (T) = 2,000 pounds
1 mile (mi) = 5,280 feet	1 gallon (gal) = 4 quarts	

Example

A roll of carpet is 11 yards 2 feet long. Is it long enough to carpet a hallway that is 32 feet long?

A. Look at the problem carefully.

What measurements do you need to compare?

11 yd 2 ft and 32 ft

B. Rename so that both measurements use the same units. If you aren't sure whether to multiply or divide, draw a picture of the units.

______ = ____ ____ ____

yd ft ft ft

THINK: Yards are larger than feet. So, **multiply** to rename yards as feet. **Divide** to rename feet as yards.

Rename the measurement that has mixed units.

11 yd = 11 x 3 **ft → 33 ft**

So, 11 yd 2 ft = 33 ft + 2 ft → 35 ft

C. Compare the measurements to solve the problem.

35 ft > 32 ft

So, the roll of carpet is long enough.

GUIDED PRACTICE

Customary Units of Measure

Units of Length	Units of Capacity	Units of Mass
1 foot (ft) = 12 inches (in.)	1 cup (c) = 8 fluid ounces (fl oz)	1 pound (lb) = 16 ounces (oz)
1 yard (yd) = 3 feet	1 quart (qt) = 4 cups	1 ton (T) = 2,000 pounds
1 mile (mi) = 5,280 feet	1 gallon (gal) = 4 quarts	

1. A truck can carry a load of 5 tons. Is it safe to load 8,000 lb of rock onto the truck?

   a. What measurements do you need to compare? 5 T and 8,000 lb

   b. Rename so that both measurements use the same units.

   THINK: When you rename a measurement in larger units, there will be fewer of them. You should **divide.**

   1 lb　　　1 ton

   Rename one measurement.

   8,000 ÷ 2,000 = 4

   c. Compare the measurements.

   4 T < 5 T

   So, it is safe to load 8,000 lb onto the truck.

2. Sarah needs to buy 9 gallons of oil. It comes in 1-quart cans. How many cans should she buy?

   a. What measurements do you need to compare?

   9 gal and 1 qt

   b. Rename so that both measurements use the same units.

   THINK: When you rename a measurement in smaller units, there will be more of them. You should **multiply.**

   Rename one measurement. Then compare measurements.

   9 x 4 = 36　　**9 gal = 36 qt**

   So, Sarah should buy 36 cans of oil.

Name ____________________

PRACTICE

Solve. Show your work. Use the table to help you change units of measurement.

Customary Units of Measurement

Units of Length	Units of Capacity	Units of Mass
1 foot (ft) = 12 inches (in.)	1 cup (c) = 8 fluid ounces (fl oz)	1 pound (lb) = 16 ounces (oz)
1 yard (yd) = 3 feet	1 quart (qt) = 4 cups	1 ton (T) = 2,000 pounds
1 mile (mi) = 5,280 feet	1 gallon (gal) = 4 quarts	

3. A serving of juice is 1 cup. **How many servings are there in 6 quarts of juice?**

   6 x 4 = 24. There are 24 servings in 6 quarts of juice.

4. A dose of cold medicine is 2 fl oz. **How many doses does a 2-cup bottle hold?**

   2 c = 2 x 8 fl oz = 16 fl oz; 16 ÷ 2 = 8. The bottle holds 8 doses.

5. A 2-ton load of bricks is delivered. The next morning, it weighs 3,800 lb. **Have bricks been added to or removed from the load?**

   2 T = 2 x 2,000 = 4,000 lb; 3,800 < 4,000. Bricks have been removed.

6. A gas tank can hold 9 gallons. **If there are 19 quarts of gas in the tank, is it more or less than half full?**

   9 gal x 4 = 36 qt; 36 ÷ 2 = 18; 19 > 18. The tank is more than half full.

7. Two boxes of rice are the same price. One contains 40 oz rice, and the other contains 2 lb 2 oz rice. **Which box is the better buy?**

   2 lb 2 oz = 32 + 2 = 34 oz; 34 < 40 The 40-oz box is the better buy.

8. A meteor's speed is measured at 10,000 feet per second. Later, its speed is 2 miles per second. **Has the meteor sped up or slowed down?**

   2 mi x 5,280 = 10,560 ft; 10,560 > 10,000. It has sped up.

TEST-TAKING PRACTICE

For questions 1–3, choose the best way to rename units for each problem. For questions 4 and 5, choose the best answer for each problem. Fill in the box of your choice in the answer section at the bottom of this page.

1. A fish tank is 26 in. long and 2 ft high. Is the tank longer than it is high? D

A $12 \div 2 = 6$ ft

B $26 - 12 = 14$ in.

C $26 \div 2 = 13$ in.

D $2 \times 12 = 24$ in.

2. A horse weighs 2,500 lb. Can it be carried in a truck that has a 2-ton weight limit? L

J $2 \times 2{,}500 = 5{,}000$ lb

K $2{,}500 \div 2 = 1{,}250$ lb

L $2 \times 2{,}000 = 4{,}000$ lb

M $2{,}500 - 2{,}000 = 500$ lb

3. Sarah is pouring 1-cup servings from 3 gallons of fruit punch. How many servings can she pour? A

A $3 \times 4 \times 4 = 48$ cups

B $3 \times 4 = 12$ cups

C $3 + 3 + 3 = 9$ cups

D $4 \times 4 \times 4 = 64$ cups

4. How many 2-ft lengths of wood can be cut from a 4-yd plank? J

J 6 L 8

K 12 M 10

5. Jerry adds 2 gal orange juice, 3 qt pineapple juice, and 1 qt soda water to make a fruit punch. How much punch does he make? B

A 4 gal C $2\frac{1}{2}$ gal

B 3 gal D 3 gal 2 qt

Write About It

Write a plan for solving the following problem. Then solve.

6. Debra is making fruit punch to sell by the cup. How many cups of punch can she sell if she makes 10 qt?

Answers will vary. Sample answer given. Rename 10 qt as cups: $10 \times 4 = 40$. Debra can sell 40 cups of punch.

1.	A ☐	B ☐	C ☐	D ☒	4.	J ☒	K ☐	L ☐	M ☐
2.	J ☐	K ☐	L ☒	M ☐	5.	A ☐	B ☒	C ☐	D ☐
3.	A ☒	B ☐	C ☐	D ☐					

Name ______________________________ **Chapter 5** L3

Deciding How to Show Measures Another Way

You often have to add, subtract, multiply, or divide in measurement problems. You may first need to decide how to show the measurements in a way that makes computing easier.

Example

A maple tree was 3 ft 5 in. tall when it was planted. The tree has now reached a height of 6 ft 3 in. How much has the tree grown?

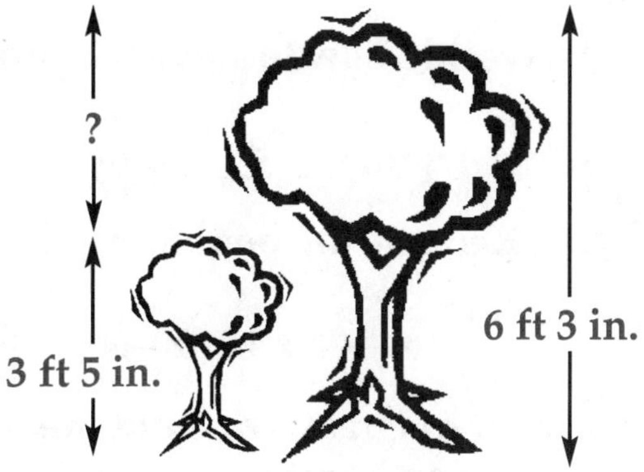

A. Make a drawing to picture the problem. You can see from the drawing that you need to subtract.

Decide how to solve the problem.

Subtract 3 ft 5 in. **from** 6 ft 3 in.**.**

B. Rename the measurements as just one unit.

6 ft → 6 x 12 **in. → 72 in.**

So, 6 ft 3 in. → 72 + 3 → 75 in.

3 ft → 3 **x 12 in. → 36 in.**

So, 3 ft 5 in. → 36 + 5 → 41 in.

On your diagram, write in the renamed measures.

C. Calculate the answer. 75 – 41 **=** 34 **in.**

So, the tree has grown 34 **in.**

GUIDED PRACTICE

1. A recipe calls for 2 ounces of peanuts per serving. How many servings can Dana make from a 3-pound bag of peanuts?

   a. Make a drawing to picture the problem. Label the measures.

   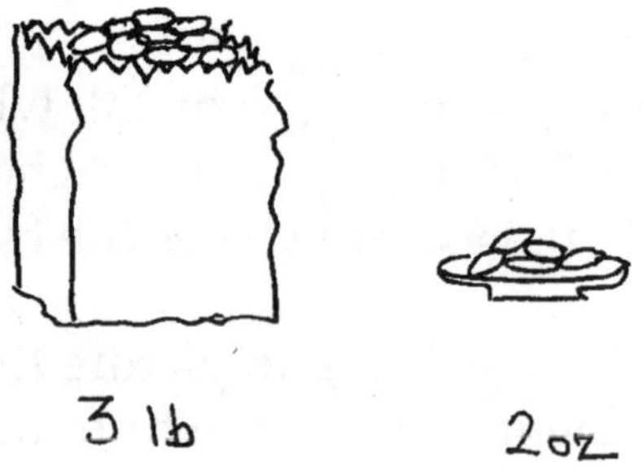

   Decide how to solve the problem.

   Divide __3__ lb by 2 oz.

   b. **Rename the pounds as ounces.**

   3 lb → 3 x 16 oz → __48__ oz

   On your diagram, cross out the pound measure, and write in the renamed measure.

   c. **Calculate the answer.**

   48 oz ÷ 2 oz = __24__

   So, Dana can make __24__ servings.

2. An empty water tank can hold 6 gallons. If each of 10 people carries a 3-qt bucket of water from a lake, can they fill the tank?

   a. **Decide how to solve the problem.**

   Multiply __3__ qt by 10.

   b. **Perform the computation.**

   3 qt x 10 = __30__ qt

   c. **Rename the quarts as gallons.**

   30 qt → 30 ÷ 4 → 7.5 gal

   d. **Compare the measurements.**

   7.5 gal > 6 gal

   So, they __can__ fill the tank.

Name ______________________

PRACTICE

Solve. Show your work. Use the table to help you rename units of measure.

Customary Units of Measure

Units of Length	Units of Capacity	Units of Mass
1 foot (ft) = 12 inches (in.)	1 cup (c) = 8 fluid ounces (fl oz)	1 pound (lb) = 16 ounces (oz)
1 yard (yd) = 3 feet	1 quart (qt) = 4 cups	1 ton (T) = 2,000 pounds
1 mile (mi) = 5,280 feet	1 gallon (gal) = 4 quarts	

3. A carpenter uses a 5 ft 4 in. length of wood for the four legs of a coffee table. How long is each leg?

   5 ft 4 in. = 64 in.; 64 in. ÷ 4 = 16 in.

   Each leg is 16 in. long.

4. Donnel is 3 in. less than 6 ft tall. How tall is he?

   Count back: 6 ft, 5 ft 11 in., 5 ft 10 in., 5 ft 9 in. Donnel is 5 ft 9 in. tall.

5. A truck weighs 3,000 lb. It is filled with 2,500 lb of gravel. Can the truck safely cross a bridge with a weight limit of 4 T?

   3,000 + 2,500 lb = 5,500 lb;

   5,500 lb < 8,000 lb. The truck can safely cross the bridge.

6. A jeweler has 1 lb 4 oz of silver to use for 5 bracelets. If each bracelet is the same, how much silver will each bracelet have?

   1 lb 4 oz = 20 oz; 20 ÷ 5 = 4.

   Each bracelet will have 4 oz silver.

7. Joe's summer tour lasts 3 weeks and 5 days. He has been touring for 1 week and 6 days. For how many more days will Joe be on tour?

   3 wk 5 d = 26 d; 1 wk 6 d = 13 d; 26 − 13 = 13. Joe will be on tour for 13 more days.

8. A chef is feeding 200 people. If she expects each person to drink 2 cups of soda, how many gallons of soda should the chef buy?

   200 x 2 = 400 c; 400 ÷ 4 = 100 qt;

   100 ÷4 = 25. The chef should buy 25 gal.

TEST-TAKING PRACTICE

Choose the best answer for each problem. In the answer section at the bottom of the page, fill in the box of your choice.

1. Four babies have the weights shown. Which baby weighs the most? C

A 288 oz　　**C** 19 lb
B 18 lb 2 oz　　**D** 300 oz

2. At a track meet, Bjorn's first jump measured 3 yd 1 ft 5 in. His second jump measured 3 yd 2 ft 3 in. How much longer was his second jump than his first? J

J 10 in.　　**L** 2 ft 2 in.
K 1 ft 10 in.　　**M** 4 ft 8 in.

3. How many cakes can Kayla bake with 3 qt of milk if each cake requires 6 fl oz of milk? B

A 10　　**C** 25
B 16　　**D** 30

4. A carpenter cuts a 2 ft 4 in. length off a plank that measured 2 yd 1 ft. How long is the plank now? J

J 4 ft 8 in.　　**L** 3 yd 4 in.
K 2 ft 4 in.　　**M** 8 in.

5. Darshana weighs 109 lb 7 oz, and her kitten weighs 3 lb 10 oz. If she stands on a scale, holding her kitten, what will the scale read? D

A 105 lb 1 oz
B 105 lb 13 oz
C 112 lb 1 oz
D 113 lb 1 oz

Write About It

Write a plan for solving the following problem. Then solve.

6. An elevator can carry a maximum weight of 1 T. Twelve people are waiting for the elevator. If each person weighs about 180 lb, can they all ride the elevator safely?

Sample answer given.

Find the total weight of the

12 people in pounds Then

compare to 2,000 lb (1 T).

12 x 180 = 2,160 lb; 2,160 > 2,000;

No, they all cannot ride safely.

1. A ☐ B ☐ C ☒ D ☐
2. J ☒ K ☐ L ☐ M ☐
3. A ☐ B ☒ C ☐ D ☐
4. J ☒ K ☐ L ☐ M ☐
5. A ☐ B ☐ C ☐ D ☒

Name ______________________________

Using Benchmarks

When you have to solve problems with fractions, look first at the denominators. If the fractions have the same denominators, you can simply compare the numerators. Otherwise, you may find it easiest to use number sense.

If the fractions in a problem have different denominators, think about how close each fraction is to 0, $\frac{1}{2}$, or 1.

- If the numerator is a small number and the denominator is a large number, the fraction is close to 0—for example: $\frac{1}{8}$, $\frac{4}{25}$, $\frac{11}{100}$.
- If the numerator is about half the denominator, the fraction is close to $\frac{1}{2}$—for example: $\frac{5}{8}$, $\frac{13}{25}$, $\frac{58}{100}$.
- If the numerator and denominator are about the same, the fraction is close to 1—for example: $\frac{7}{8}$, $\frac{23}{25}$, $\frac{97}{100}$.

Example

Mrs. Wong wants the widest wallpaper border. Which of the three borders is the widest?

Border	Width
solid	$2\frac{5}{8}$ in.
geometric	$2\frac{13}{16}$ in.
flowered	$2\frac{1}{4}$ in.

A. First, compare the whole-number parts of the three mixed numbers. **Is there any difference among the whole-number parts of the fractions?**

no

B. If the whole-number parts are the same, compare the fraction parts.

THINK: 5 is about half of 8. So, $\frac{5}{8}$ is close to $\frac{1}{2}$.

13 and 16 are about the same. So, $\frac{13}{16}$ is close to 1.

1 is much smaller than 4. So, $\frac{1}{4}$ is close to 0.

C. Now use your approximations with the mixed numbers.

$2\frac{5}{8}$ is close to $2\frac{1}{2}$.

$2\frac{13}{16}$ is close to 3.

$2\frac{1}{4}$ is close to 2.

D. Compare the approximations.

Which mixed number is greatest? $2\frac{13}{16}$

So, the geometric **border is the widest.**

GUIDED PRACTICE

1. Jenny and Troy see this sign at the Visitor's Center of an amusement park. Which is closer to the Visitor's Center, Dinosaur Village or the Water Slide?

Visitor's Center
Dinosaur Village... $\frac{3}{8}$ mi →
← Water Slide... $\frac{9}{10}$ mi

Step 1: Write down the distances you will compare.

Dinosaur Village is $\frac{3}{8}$ mi from the Visitor's Center.

The Water Slide is $\frac{9}{10}$ mi from the Visitor's Center.

Step 2: Use benchmarks to compare the fractions.

Is $\frac{3}{8}$ closest to 0, $\frac{1}{2}$, or 1? $\frac{1}{2}$

Is $\frac{9}{10}$ closest to 0, $\frac{1}{2}$, or 1? 1

Step 3: Compare the approximations from Step 2.

$\frac{1}{2} < 1$. So, $\frac{3}{8} < \frac{9}{10}$.

So, Dinosaur Village **is closer to the visitor's center.**

2. Fred wants to hike on the longest trail. He reads the sign at the right. Which trail should he take?

Red Trail	$4\frac{5}{8}$ mi
Yellow Trail	$4\frac{1}{2}$ mi
Blue Trail	$5\frac{1}{8}$ mi

Step 1: Write down the distances you will compare.

Red Trail is $4\frac{5}{8}$ mi long.

Yellow Trail is $4\frac{1}{2}$ mi long.

Blue Trail is $5\frac{1}{8}$ mi long.

Step 2: Compare the mixed numbers.

Which whole number is greatest? 5

Step 3: If one of the whole-number parts is greatest, that mixed number is the greatest. You don't have to compare the fractions.

Which trail is longest? the Blue Trail

So, Fred should take the Blue **Trail.**

Name ______________________ **Chapter 6** **L1**

PRACTICE

Solve. Use benchmark fractions to help you.

3. **A store is displaying three bookshelves in order from least to greatest height. The heights of the bookshelves are $4\frac{1}{6}$ ft, $4\frac{7}{8}$ ft, and $4\frac{5}{12}$ ft. In which order will the store display the shelves?**

   $4\frac{1}{6}$ ft, $4\frac{5}{12}$ ft, $4\frac{7}{8}$ ft

4. **Linda wants to bake a pie. The recipe calls for about $1\frac{1}{2}$ lb of cherries. At the grocery store, there are bags of cherries weighing $1\frac{7}{16}$ lb, $1\frac{7}{8}$ lb, and 2 lb. Which of the three bags should Linda buy?**

   the $1\frac{7}{16}$-lb bag

5. **Three bags of grass seed at the store all sell for the same price. The bags weigh $7\frac{1}{4}$ lb, $7\frac{5}{8}$ lb, and $6\frac{7}{8}$ lb. Which of the bags is the best buy?**

   the $7\frac{5}{8}$-lb bag

6. **Shelly has rolled-up ribbons labeled with these lengths: $3\frac{7}{8}$ ft, $3\frac{1}{4}$ ft, and $3\frac{7}{12}$ ft. If she wants to use the longest ribbon to hem a skirt, which ribbon should she use?**

   the $3\frac{7}{8}$-ft ribbon

7. **Jake needs a rod to fit tightly into a hole with a diameter of 2 in. The hardware store has rods with the following diameters: $2\frac{1}{8}$ in., $1\frac{1}{4}$ in., $1\frac{3}{16}$ in., $1\frac{7}{8}$ in., and $1\frac{7}{16}$ in. Which rod will fit the hole most tightly?**

   the $1\frac{7}{8}$-in. rod

8. **Jorge is tired from hiking and wants to take the shortest route back to camp. The Willow Trail is $1\frac{3}{10}$-km long. The Forest Trail is $2\frac{1}{5}$-km long, and the Pond Trail is $1\frac{7}{8}$-km long. Which of the trails should he take back?**

   the Willow Trail

9. **A scientist has four drums of the same chemical. The drums hold $7\frac{3}{32}$ gallons, $7\frac{9}{16}$ gallons, $6\frac{31}{32}$ gallons, and $7\frac{7}{16}$ gallons. Which of the drums holds the most?**

   the $7\frac{9}{16}$-gallon drum

10. **Three athletes competed in a long-jump event. Stephen's jump measured $11\frac{7}{12}$ ft. Johanne's jump measured $12\frac{1}{4}$ ft, and Raiku's jump measured $11\frac{5}{6}$ ft. Which of the athletes won the event?**

    Johanne

TEST-TAKING PRACTICE

For problems 1–5, choose the best answer for each problem. In the answer section at the bottom of the page, fill in the box of your choice.

1. An electrician has lengths of wire measuring $3\frac{1}{8}$ ft, $2\frac{3}{4}$ ft, $3\frac{5}{8}$ ft, and $3\frac{11}{12}$ ft. **If he wants to use the longest piece, which should he pick?** D
   - **A** $3\frac{1}{8}$ ft
   - **B** $2\frac{3}{4}$ ft
   - **C** $3\frac{5}{8}$ ft
   - **D** $3\frac{11}{12}$ ft

2. Donna needs about 2 lb of peanuts for a recipe. **Which of the following weights is closest to 2 lb?** K
   - **J** $2\frac{7}{16}$ lb
   - **K** $1\frac{7}{8}$ lb
   - **L** $2\frac{1}{2}$ lb
   - **M** 3 lb

3. In the high jump, Pablo jumped 7 ft $5\frac{9}{16}$ in. Sam jumped 7 ft $4\frac{1}{12}$ in. Jeff jumped 7 ft $5\frac{11}{12}$ in. Alan jumped 7 ft $5\frac{7}{12}$ in. **Who jumped the highest?** C
   - **A** Pablo
   - **B** Sam
   - **C** Jeff
   - **D** Alan

4. **Why is the fraction $\frac{8}{15}$ close to $\frac{1}{2}$?** M
   - **J** The numerator and the denominator are about the same.
   - **K** The numerator is a small number.
   - **L** The numerator is close to twice the denominator.
   - **M** The numerator is close to half the denominator.

5. A dinosaur's leg bones can be clues to the size of the dinosaur. The longest bones usually come from the longest dinosaurs.

   Which one of the following leg bones probably came from the longest dinosaur? A
   - **A** Bone A: $6\frac{9}{10}$ ft
   - **B** Bone B: $6\frac{1}{5}$ ft
   - **C** Bone C: $6\frac{7}{10}$ ft
   - **D** Bone D: $6\frac{1}{2}$ ft

Write About It

Write a plan for solving the following problem. Then solve.

6. **The three winning throws in a javelin-throwing contest were $75\frac{1}{8}$ yd, $74\frac{15}{16}$ yd, and $74\frac{3}{8}$ yd. Which throw earned second place?**

   Sample answer: Compare the whole-number parts of the mixed numbers first. Then use benchmarks to compare the fraction parts. Order the numbers. The $74\frac{15}{16}$-yd throw earned second place.

1. A ☐ B ☐ C ☐ D ☒
2. J ☐ K ☒ L ☐ M ☐
3. A ☐ B ☐ C ☒ D ☐
4. J ☐ K ☐ L ☐ M ☒
5. A ☒ B ☐ C ☐ D ☐

Name ____________________ **Chapter 6 L2**

Drawing a Number Line

To solve some problems, you'll have to add and subtract fractions. Drawing a number line to show the information can help you.

Example

The ceiling in Josh's room is 8 ft high. There is a shelf $5\frac{5}{6}$ ft above the floor. Can Josh place a painting that is $2\frac{1}{2}$ ft tall on the shelf?

A. Decide what you need to find out.

Is the sum of $5\frac{5}{6}$ and $2\frac{1}{2}$ less than ___8___?

B. Use benchmarks to approximate the larger number.

$\frac{5}{6}$ is close to 1. So, $5\frac{5}{6}$ is close to ___6___.

C. Draw a number line.

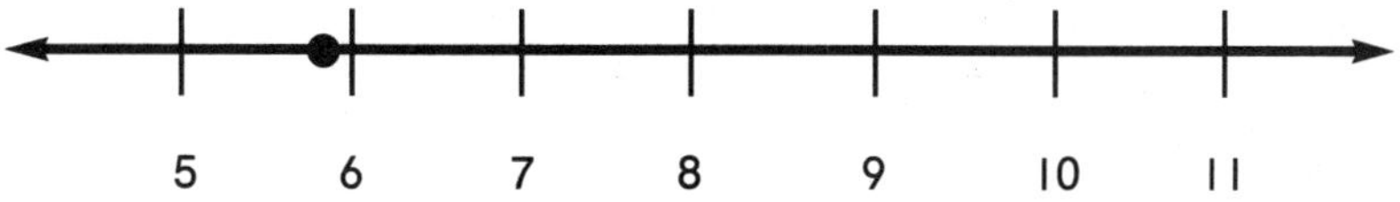

Mark the line with a dot a little to the left of 6.

D. Use benchmarks to approximate the smaller number.

$\frac{1}{2}$ is equal to $\frac{1}{2}$. So, use ___$2\frac{1}{2}$___ as the smaller number.

E. Use the number line to count on from the dot.

Move $2\frac{1}{2}$ spaces to the right.

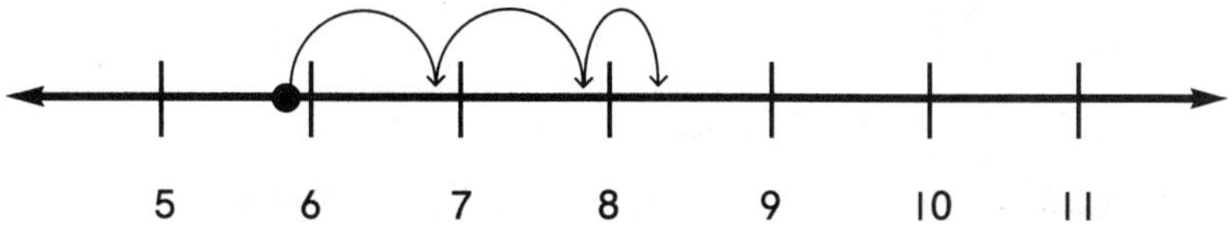

Does the point show less or more than 8? ___more than 8___

So, Josh ___cannot___ **place the painting on the shelf.**

GUIDED PRACTICE

1. Dolores needs 5 lb of apples for a recipe. She split a bag of apples weighing $7\frac{5}{8}$ lb with Ralph, and gave him $2\frac{3}{16}$ lb of the apples. Does Dolores have enough apples left for her recipe?

Step 1: Decide what you need to find out.

Is the difference of $7\frac{5}{8}$ and $2\frac{3}{16}$ greater than __5__?

Step 2: Draw a number line.

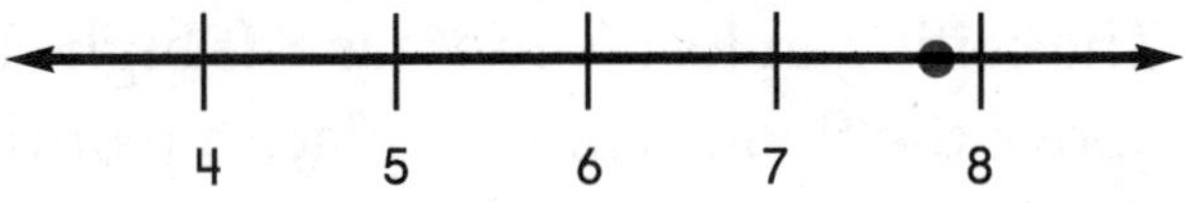

THINK: $7\frac{5}{8}$ is a little more than $7\frac{1}{2}$.

Mark the line with a dot a little to the right of $7\frac{1}{2}$.

Step 3: Use the number line to count down.

THINK: $2\frac{3}{16}$ is a little more than 2.

Move a little more than 2 spaces to the left.

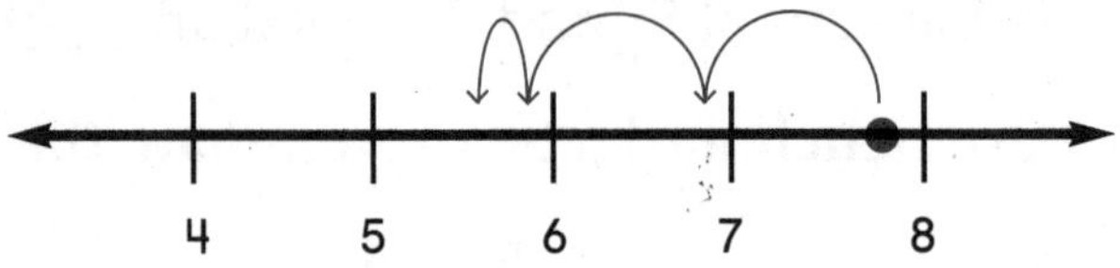

Does the point show less or more than 5?

__more than 5__

So, Dolores __has__ enough apples.

2. A scientist mixes $3\frac{1}{3}$ pt of one liquid to $1\frac{1}{6}$ pt of another liquid. How many pints of the mixture does she have?

Step 1: Decide what you need to find out.

What is the sum of __$3\frac{1}{3}$__ and __$1\frac{1}{6}$__?

Step 2: You need an exact answer.

Can you use a number line? __No__

Write the numbers as equivalent fractions, and add.

$3\frac{2}{6} + 1\frac{1}{6} = 4\frac{3}{6}$

THINK: I can simplify $\frac{3}{6}$ to $\frac{1}{2}$.

So, the scientist has __$4\frac{1}{2}$__ pt of the mixture.

Check your answer on a number line. Mark a dot just to the left of $3\frac{1}{2}$. Move right a little more than 1 space.

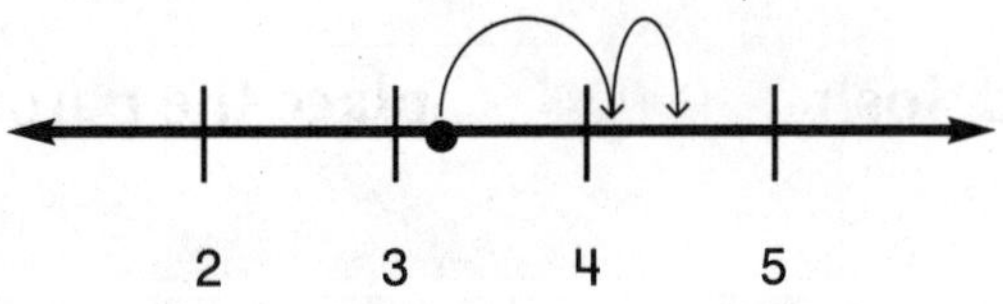

Name ____________________

PRACTICE

Mark on the number line to solve each problem.

3. **Bill has two containers of water. One container has $5\frac{1}{8}$ pt, and the other has $2\frac{7}{12}$ pt. Can he pour both into an 8-pt bucket without its overflowing?**

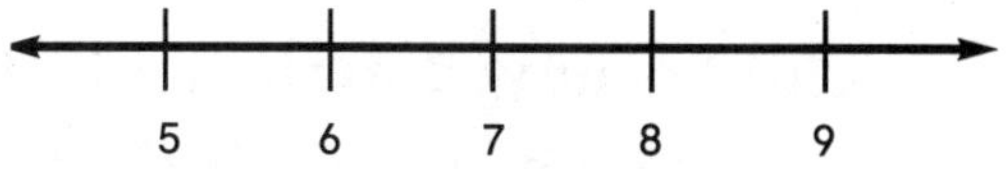

Yes

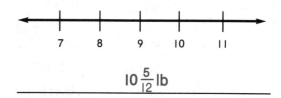

4. **A table is $3\frac{11}{12}$ ft wide, and a couch is $6\frac{2}{3}$ ft wide. Will they fit side by side along a wall that is 10 ft long?**

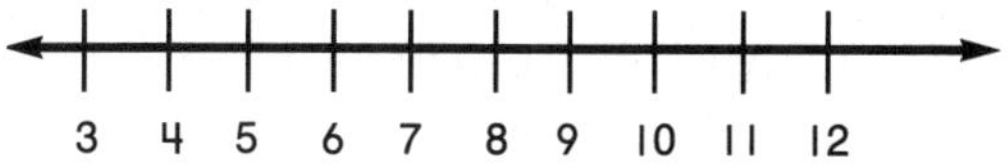

No

5. **A jeweler has $9\frac{9}{16}$ oz of silver. He uses $4\frac{7}{8}$ oz for a bracelet. He wants to make a necklace that will take 5 oz of silver. Does he have enough left?**

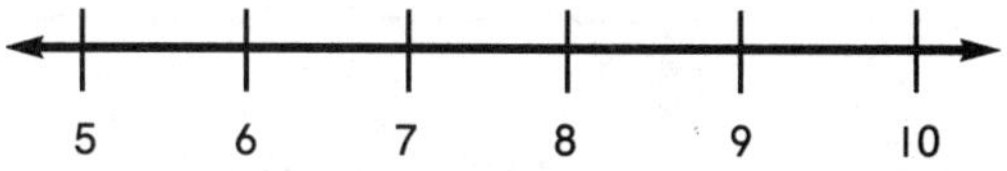

No

Find the LCD to solve. Use a number line to check your answer.

6. **A baby weighed $7\frac{1}{4}$ lb at birth. By the following January, the baby had gained $3\frac{1}{6}$ lb. How much did the baby weigh in January?**

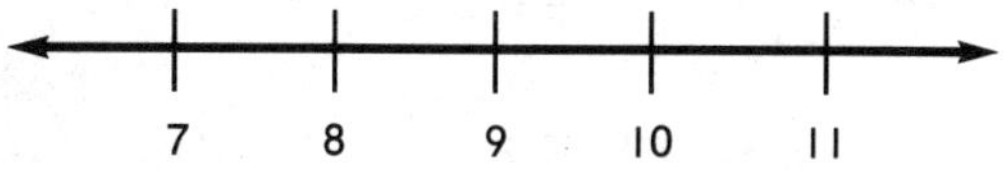

$10\frac{5}{12}$ lb

7. **An electrician uses a $4\frac{5}{8}$ ft length from a roll of $10\frac{11}{12}$ ft of wire. What length of wire does she have left?**

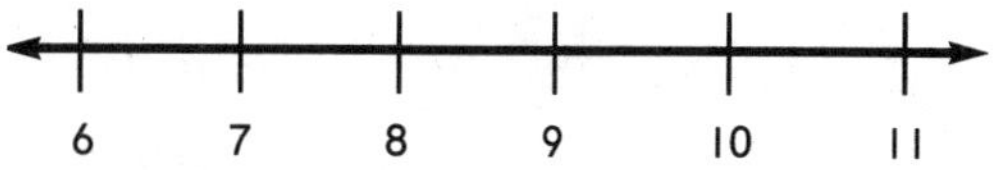

$6\frac{7}{24}$ ft

8. **Two hiking trails measure $4\frac{3}{10}$ miles and $3\frac{1}{4}$ miles long. How many miles does Sven travel if he hikes both trails?**

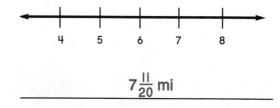

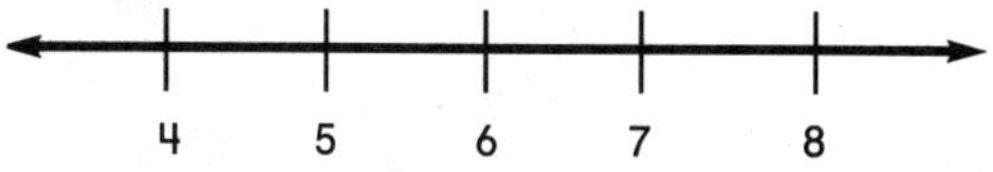

$7\frac{11}{20}$ mi

TEST-TAKING PRACTICE

Choose the best answer for each problem. In the answer section at the bottom of the page, fill in the box of your choice.

1. A tree was $5\frac{1}{6}$ ft tall two years ago. Since then, it has grown $4\frac{3}{8}$ ft taller. Which of the following statements is true? A

A The tree is less than 10 ft tall.
B The tree is more than 10 ft tall.
C The tree is exactly 10 ft tall.
D The tree is exactly 9 ft tall.

2. Haruko took $1\frac{11}{12}$ lb of sugar from a bag that contained $4\frac{3}{8}$ lb of sugar. Which of the following statements is true? K

J The bag has less than 2 lb of sugar.
K The bag has about $2\frac{1}{2}$ lb of sugar.
L The bag has about 3 lb of sugar.
M The bag has about $6\frac{1}{2}$ lb of sugar.

3. Sam pours $5\frac{3}{4}$ gallons of gas into a tank that already contains $1\frac{1}{8}$ gallons. How much gas is in the tank? C

A $4\frac{5}{8}$ gal　　C $6\frac{7}{8}$ gal
B $6\frac{5}{8}$ gal　　D 7 gal

4. A carpenter has a board that is $8\frac{2}{3}$ ft long. She cuts a $4\frac{1}{6}$ ft length off the board. How long is the remaining piece? J

J $4\frac{1}{2}$ ft　　L 5 ft
K $4\frac{5}{6}$ ft　　M $12\frac{5}{6}$ ft

5. A child is now double her birth length. If she was $20\frac{1}{8}$ inches long at birth, how tall is she now? C

A $22\frac{1}{8}$ in.　　C $40\frac{1}{4}$ in.
B $40\frac{1}{8}$ in.　　D $40\frac{1}{2}$ in.

Write About It

6. Explain how you can estimate answers to problems with fractions by using a number line.

Use benchmarks to approximate the fractions. Mark a number line with one of the numbers, and then move the same number of spaces as the other number—to the right to add or to the left to subtract.

1. A ☒ B ☐ C ☐ D ☐
2. J ☐ K ☒ L ☐ M ☐
3. A ☐ B ☐ C ☒ D ☐
4. J ☒ K ☐ L ☐ M ☐
5. A ☐ B ☐ C ☒ D ☐

Name ____________________

Test-Taking Skill: Writing a Plan

On some tests, you need to explain how to solve a problem. It is important to explain your thinking and to show your calculations.

Example

Kelly's television uses 0.20 kilowatt-hour of electricity every hour that it is on. She pays $0.12 for each kilowatt-hour. About how much does it cost to run her television for 4 hours?

A. Read the problem carefully. Decide on the kind of answer you need.

The answer is the amount of money it costs to run the television for 4 hours.

B. Write a plan for finding the answer.

1: First, I will find how much one hour of television costs by multiplying the number of kilowatt-hours by the cost per kilowatt-hour.

2: Then, I will multiply that product by 4 to find about how much 4 hours costs.

C. Follow your plan, and solve the problem. Show your calculations.

1:	$ 0.12	Cost per kilowatt-hour
	x 0.20	Number of kilowatt-hours per hour of TV use
	$ 0.024	Cost to run TV for one hour
2:	$ 0.024	Cost to run TV for one hour
	x 4	Number of hours of TV use
	$ 0.096	Cost to run TV for 4 hours

Money amounts need to be written to two decimal places. You need to round $ 0.096 up to $ 0.10.

So, it costs Kelly about $ 0.10 for 4 hours of television.

TEST-TAKING PRACTICE

Write a plan to solve each problem. Explain your thinking and show your calculations. Then solve the problem.

1. Paul's air conditioner uses 36 kilowatt-hours of electricity a day. He had it on for 6 days straight in July. Paul pays $0.13 a kilowatt-hour.

How much did he pay for those 6 days of air-conditioning?

First, multiply the cost per kilowatt-hour by the number of kilowatt-hours to find out how much it costs to run the air conditioner for 1 day. Then, multiply that product by the number of days to find the total cost.

36 x $0.13 = $4.68

6 x $4.68 = $28.08

Paul paid $28.08 for 6 days of air-conditioning.

2. Three classes are taking a field-trip. Mr. De Marco's class has 27 students. Ms. De Fabbia's class has 32 students. Mrs. Lawrence's class has 28 students. Each bus for their trip has 45 seats.

Can all three classes and their teachers fit in 2 buses?

First, add to find the total number of students in all three classes plus the 3 teachers. Next, multiply the seats on the bus by 2. Then, compare the number of seats to the number of passengers.

27 + 32 + 28 = 87.

87 + 3 = 90.

2 x 45 = 90. There are 90 passengers and 90 seats. So, all three classes can fit into 2 buses.

Drawing a Picture to Rename Measures

Some problems require you to rename measures given as a fraction of one unit. You can find the information you need in a table. It often helps to draw a picture of the unit you are renaming.

Customary Units of Measure

Units of Length	Units of Capacity	Units of Mass
1 foot (ft) = 12 inches (in.)	1 cup (c) = 8 fluid ounces (fl oz)	1 pound (lb) = 16 ounces (oz)
1 yard (yd) = 36 inches	1 pint (pt) = 2 cups (c)	1 ton (T) = 2,000 pounds
1 yard = 3 feet	1 quart (qt) = 2 pints	
1 mile (mi) = 5,280 feet	1 gallon (gal) = 4 quarts	
1 mile = 1,760 yards		

Example

The soccer team brought $2\frac{1}{2}$ gallons of orange juice. Each player will get 1 pint of juice. How many players can have orange juice?

A. Find the number of pints in a gallon. If the table doesn't compare gallons and pints, find a unit that is compared to both gallons and pints.

Draw pictures of equivalent amounts of each of the units.

1 gal = __4__ qt   1 qt = __2__ pt

1 gal → 4 x 2 pt → __8__ pt

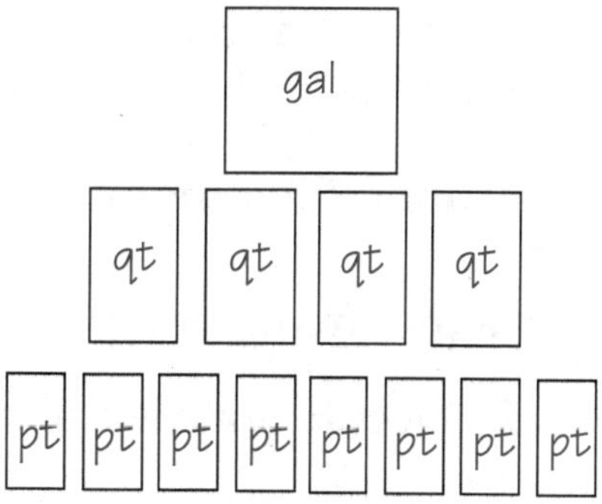

B. Decide whether to multiply or divide when you rename the units.

- **Multiply** to rename a larger unit as a smaller unit.
- **Divide** to rename a smaller unit as a larger unit.

THINK: Pints are smaller, so there will be more pints than gallons.

To rename gallons as pints, you should __multiply__.

C. Compute to solve the problem.

Number of gallons x pints per gallon = total pints

$2\frac{1}{2}$ x __8__ = __20__

So, __20__ players can have orange juice.

GUIDED PRACTICE

1. Tara has $1\frac{1}{2}$ quarts of apple cider. How many cups can she serve?

Step 1: Find the number of cups in a quart. Draw a picture if it helps you.

1 qt = __2__ pt   1 pt = __2__ c

1 qt → 2 x 2 c → __4__ c

Step 2: Decide whether to multiply or divide when you rename the units.

THINK: There will be more cups than quarts.

To rename quarts as cups, you should __multiply__.

Step 3: Compute to solve the problem.

Number of quarts x cups per quart = total cups

$1\frac{1}{2}$ x 4 = 6

So, Tara can serve __6__ cups of apple cider.

2. A window is 76 inches high. Will a curtain $6\frac{1}{2}$ ft long cover the window?

Step 1: Find the number of inches in a foot.

Draw a picture if it helps you. 1 ft = __12__ in.

Step 2: Decide whether to multiply or divide to rename the units.

THINK: There will be fewer feet than inches.

To rename inches as feet, you should __divide__.

Step 3: Compute to rename the measure.

Number of inches ÷ inches per foot = total feet

76 ÷ 12 = $6\frac{1}{3}$

Compare the measures. $6\frac{1}{3}$ ft < $6\frac{1}{2}$ ft

So, the curtain __will__ cover the window.

Name ________________________________ **Chapter 7** L1

PRACTICE

Solve. Use the table of measures to find the information you need. Draw pictures if they help you.

Customary Units of Measure

Units of Length	Units of Capacity	Units of Mass
1 foot (ft) = 12 inches (in.)	1 cup (c) = 8 fluid ounces (fl oz)	1 pound (lb) = 16 ounces (oz)
1 yard (yd) = 36 inches	1 pint (pt) = 2 cups	1 ton (T) = 2,000 pounds
1 yard = 3 feet	1 quart (qt) = 2 pints	
1 mile (mi) = 5,280 feet	1 gallon = 4 quarts	
1 mile = 1,760 yards		

3. **Janine has $\frac{2}{3}$ ft of red ribbon. How many inches of trim can she sew with the ribbon?**

   $\frac{2}{3} \times 12 = 8$ in.

4. **Kelly's favorite tree is 22 ft high. Will an $8\frac{1}{3}$-yd ladder reach the top of the tree?**

   25 ft > 22 ft. Yes, the ladder will reach.

5. **Gina is installing a TV cable $5\frac{1}{3}$ yd long. How many feet will the cable stretch?**

   $5\frac{1}{3} \times 3 = 16$ ft

6. **A truck can carry a maximum weight of $3\frac{1}{2}$ tons. Can it carry 7,500 pounds of gravel?**

   7,000 < 7,500. No, it cannot.

7. **Robert pours $4\frac{3}{4}$ qt of lemonade into cups. How many cups does he fill?**

   $4\frac{3}{4} \times 4 = 19$ c

8. **Joan built a fence 14 ft long. She charges for her work by the yard. How many yards long is the fence?**

   $14 \div 3 = 4\frac{2}{3}$ yd

9. **The road to Alec's house is $2\frac{1}{2}$ miles long. There are markers every 100 yards along the road. How many markers are there?**

   4,400 ÷ 100 = 44 markers

10. **Two bags of flour sell for the same price. One weighs $1\frac{1}{4}$ lb, and the other weighs 22 oz. Which is the better buy?**

    22 > 20. The 22-oz bag is a better buy.

TEST-TAKING PRACTICE

For problems 1–4, choose the best answer for each problem. In the answer section at the bottom of the page, fill in the box of your choice.

Customary Units of Measurements

Units of Length	Units of Capacity	Units of Mass
1 foot (ft) = 12 inches (in.)	1 cup (c) = 8 fluid ounces (fl oz)	1 pound (lb) = 16 ounces (oz)
1 yard (yd) = 36 inches	1 pint (pt) = 2 cups	1 ton (T) = 2,000 pounds
1 yard (yd) = 3 feet	1 quart (qt) = 2 pints	
1 mile (mi) = 5,280 feet	1 gallon (gal) = 4 quarts	
1 mile = 1,760 yards		

1. How many pint bottles can be filled with 64 fl oz of water? B

A 2   C 16
B 4   D 64

2. The gym teacher is marking off a $\frac{1}{2}$-mi track. How many yards long should the track be? K

J 440 yd   L 1,760 yd
K 880 yd   M 3,520 yd

3. A length of fabric is $4\frac{1}{2}$ ft long and 50 inches wide. Which statement is true? B

A It is wider than it is long.
B It is longer than it is wide.
C Its length equals its width.
D Its width is half its length.

4. Which of the following number sentences can you use to find the number of cups in 1 gallon? L

J 2 x 2 = 4 cups
K 2 x 4 = 8 cups
L 2 x 2 x 4 = 16 cups
M 8 x 2 x 2 = 32 cups

Write About It

Write a plan for solving the following problem. Then solve.

5. Duane jumped $3\frac{3}{4}$ yd and Momo jumped 11 ft 5 in. Who jumped farther?

Find how many inches are in each measurement by multiplying. Then compare the number of inches.

$3\frac{3}{4} \times 36 = 135$ $11 \times 12 = 132$

$132 + 5 = 137$ $137 > 135$

Momo jumped farther.

1. A ☐ B ☒ C ☐ D ☐
2. J ☐ K ☒ L ☐ M ☐
3. A ☐ B ☒ C ☐ D ☐
4. J ☐ K ☐ L ☒ M ☐

Name ____________________

Is the Computed Number the Answer?

When you compute to solve a problem, the result of the computation is often the answer. Sometimes, you must decide whether the computation gives the kind of answer you need.

Example 1

It takes $1\frac{1}{2}$ cups of flour to make one batch of muffins. How many batches of muffins can you make with 5 cups of flour?

A. Divide the total amount of flour by the amount it takes to make one batch of muffins.

$5 \div \underline{1\frac{1}{2}} = \underline{3\frac{1}{3}}$

B. Reread the problem to determine if the quotient is the answer to the problem.

THINK: The problem asks how many *batches* you can make.

Does it make sense to have $3\frac{1}{3}$ batches of muffins? Yes

So, $3\frac{1}{3}$ batches of muffins is the answer to the problem.

Example 2

A storm is threatening an island. Rescue boats can carry 8 people at a time. How many boats will the 43 people on the island need?

Step 1: Divide the total number of people by the number of people per boat.

$43 \div \underline{8} = \underline{5\frac{3}{8}}$

Step 2: Reread the problem. Is the quotient the answer to the problem?

THINK: **Does it make sense to have $5\frac{3}{8}$ boats?** No

Step 3: If the quotient doesn't answer the problem sensibly, round up or down.

THINK: All the people need boats, so you need to round up.

Round the quotient up to the next whole number.

So, the people on the island will need 6 **boats.**

GUIDED PRACTICE

1. Maria needs 15 quarts of fruit punch for a party. The punch is sold in 2-quart bottles. How many bottles should she buy?

   Step 1: Divide the total number of quarts by the number of quarts per bottle.

   $15 \div \underline{\quad 2 \quad} = \underline{\quad 7\frac{1}{2} \quad}$

   Step 2: Reread the problem to determine whether the quotient is the correct answer.

   Can Maria buy $7\frac{1}{2}$ bottles of punch? ___No___

   Step 3: If the quotient doesn't answer the problem sensibly, round up or down.

   THINK: Maria needs 15 quarts, so I need to round up.

   Round the quotient up to the next whole number.

   Maria should buy ___8___ **bottles of punch.**

2. A recipe calls for 4 oz of chicken per person served. How many people can Rue serve if she has 18 oz of chicken?

   Step 1: Divide the total ounces of chicken by the ounces per serving.

   $18 \div \underline{\quad 4 \quad} = \underline{\quad 4\frac{1}{2} \quad}$

   Step 2: Reread the problem to determine whether the quotient is the correct answer.

   Can Rue serve $4\frac{1}{2}$ people? ___No___

   Step 3: If the quotient doesn't answer the problem sensibly, round up or down.

   THINK: Each person needs a whole serving, so I need to round down.

   Round the quotient down to the next whole number.

   So, Rue can serve ___4___ **people.**

Name ______________________

PRACTICE

Decide which kind of answer makes the most sense for each problem. Then solve.

3. **Alina is sewing shirts. She has 8 yards of fabric. If 1 shirt takes $2\frac{1}{2}$ yd of fabric, how many shirts can she make?**

   3 shirts

4. **A video store is moving and packing its tapes into boxes. Each box holds 80 videos. How many boxes are needed for the store's 5,432 tapes?**

   68 boxes

5. **Juice boxes come in packages of 3 boxes each. How many packages should Mr. Lopez buy if he wants 1 box for each of his 26 scouts?**

   9 packages

6. **The Juice Bar gives customers 1 free drink for every 5 drinks they buy in one month. How many free drinks can Tim get if he buys 17 drinks this month?**

   3 free drinks

7. **Eddie has 245 baseball cards. Each page in his binder can hold 9 cards. How many pages does Eddie need for all of his cards?**

   28 pages

8. **A space taxi uses 6 gallons of fuel for each passenger it carries between stations. If the taxi has 35 gallons of fuel, how many passengers can it carry?**

   5 passengers

9. **After their matches, 4 soccer teams have pizza delivered. They have 18 pizzas to share. How many pizzas can each team have?**

   $4\frac{1}{2}$ pizzas

10. **A factory produces a new car every $3\frac{1}{2}$ hours. How many cars does the factory produce in a 40-hour week?**

    11 cars

TEST-TAKING PRACTICE

For problems 1–6, choose the best solution for each problem. In the answer section at the bottom of the page, fill in the box of your choice.

1. A bus holds 44 passengers. How many buses are needed to take 286 people on a trip? C

A 6 **C** 7

B $6\frac{1}{2}$ **D** $7\frac{1}{2}$

2. Luis feeds his puppy 4 oz of food at each meal. How many meals can Luis give the puppy from a 50-oz bag of food? J

J 12 **L** 13

K $12\frac{1}{2}$ **M** 46

3. A restaurant owner is feeding 250 people. She needs a slice of pie for each person. Each pie is cut into 8 slices. How many pies should she order? C

A 16 **C** 32

B 31 **D** 125

4. A jogger runs 4 days a week. This week, she ran 15 miles. What was the average number of miles she ran per day? K

J 3 **L** 4

K $3\frac{3}{4}$ **M** 9

5. A truck can hold 4,000 lb. Each box of machine parts weighs 35 lb. How many boxes can the truck hold? B

A 14 **C** $114\frac{1}{3}$

B 114 **D** 115

6. It takes 3 people to crew a sailing boat in a contest. How many boats can a club enter in the contest if there are 26 members? J

J 8 **L** 9

K $8\frac{2}{3}$ **M** 23

Write About It

Write a plan for solving the following problem. Then solve.

7. A carpenter bought a board that was 10 ft long. He plans to cut it into shelves that are $1\frac{1}{2}$ feet long. How many shelves can he make?

Divide the length of the board by the length of each shelf. Then decide whether the computed answer is sensible or whether it should be rounded up or down.

$10 \div 1\frac{1}{2} = 6\frac{2}{3}$. Round down, because $\frac{2}{3}$ of a shelf is not reasonable. He can make 6 shelves.

1.	A ☐	B ☐	C ☒	D ☐
2.	J ☒	K ☐	L ☐	M ☐
3.	A ☐	B ☐	C ☒	D ☐
4.	J ☐	K ☒	L ☐	M ☐
5.	A ☐	B ☒	C ☐	D ☐
6.	J ☒	K ☐	L ☐	M ☐

Name ____________________

Using Models

In some problems, you'll have to divide whole numbers by fractions. You may find it helpful to use a model.

Example 1

A box contains 3 cups of cereal. If one serving of cereal is $\frac{3}{4}$ cup, how many servings does the box contain?

A. **Draw three rectangles to represent 3 cups.**

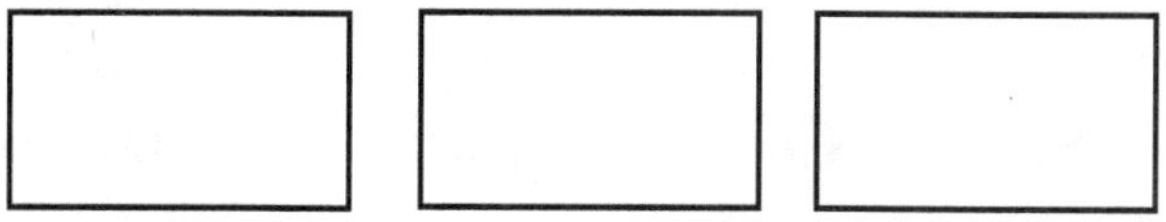

B. **The divisor, $\frac{3}{4}$, is in fourths. So, divide the rectangles into fourths.**

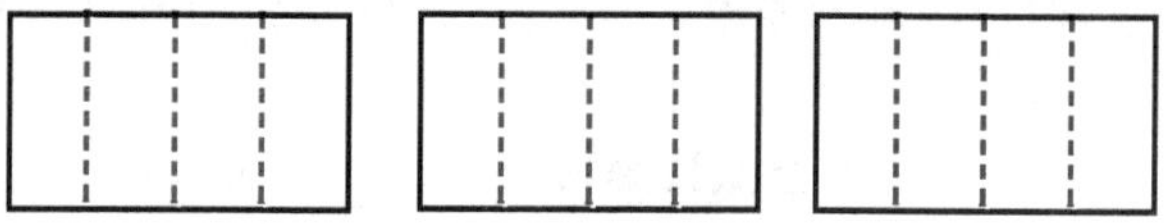

C. Count how many groups of $\frac{3}{4}$ fit into the rectangles.

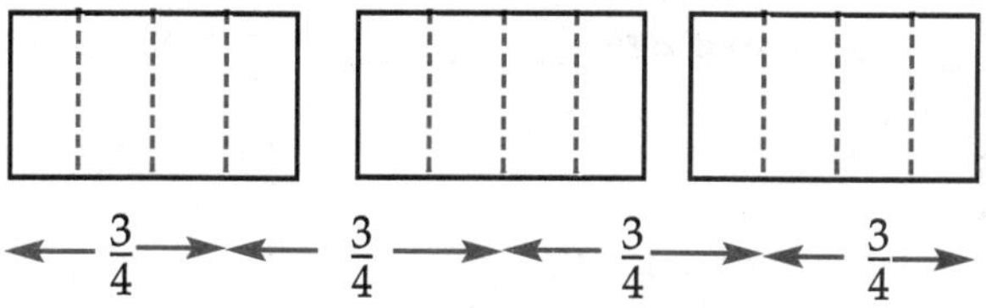

How many groups of $\frac{3}{4}$ fit?

__4__ **groups**

So, the box contains __4__ servings.

Example 2

Mr. Woo has 4 ft of aluminum foil. He wants to cut pieces that are $\frac{1}{3}$ ft long. How many pieces can he cut?

Step 1: Draw four rectangles to represent 4 feet.

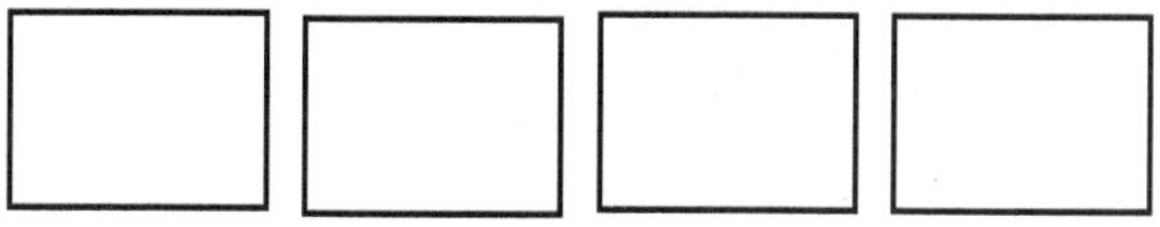

Step 2: The divisor, $\frac{1}{3}$, is in thirds.

Divide the rectangles into thirds.

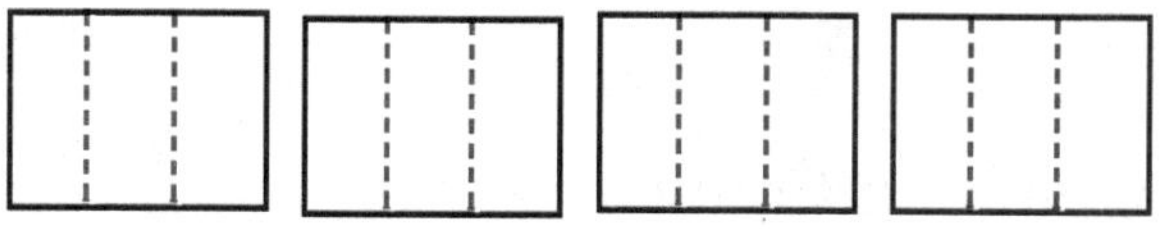

Step 3: Count the number of thirds.

THINK: There are 3 pieces in each foot.

So, I can multiply 4 x 3. **4 x 3 =** __12__

So, Mr. Woo can cut __12__ **pieces.**

GUIDED PRACTICE

1. A wooden fence is 5 yd long. Each section is $\frac{1}{2}$ yd long. How many sections of fence are there?

Step 1: Draw five rectangles to represent 5 yards.

Step 2: Divide the rectangles into halves.

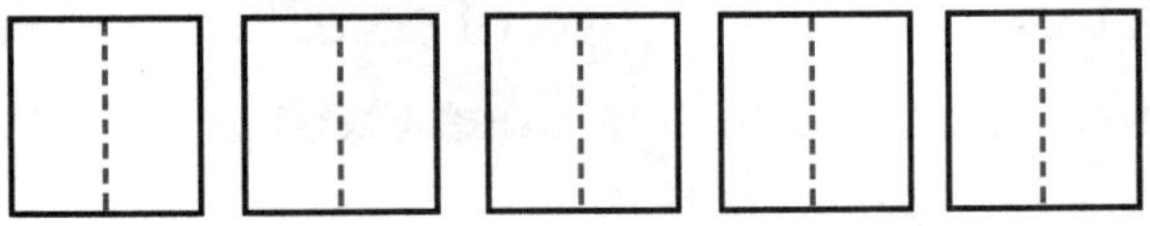

Step 3: Count the number of halves.

THINK: There are 2 sections in each yard.

So, I can multiply 5 x 2.   5 x 2 = __10__

So, there are __10__ sections of fence.

2. Rita has 4 pints of juice. One serving is $\frac{2}{3}$ pt. How many servings of juice does she have?

Step 1: Draw four rectangles to represent 4 pints.

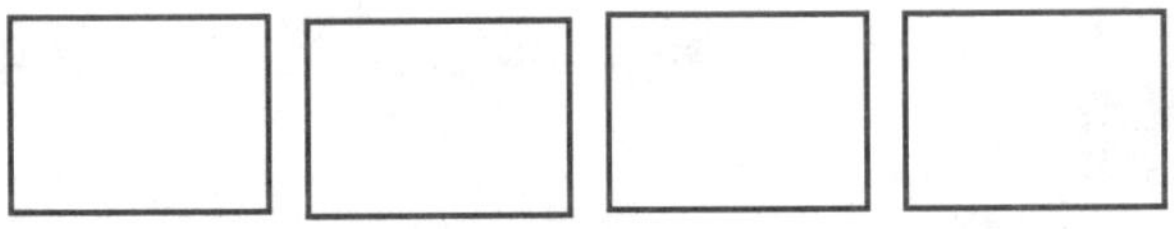

Step 2: The divisor, $\frac{2}{3}$, is in thirds. So, divide the rectangles into thirds.

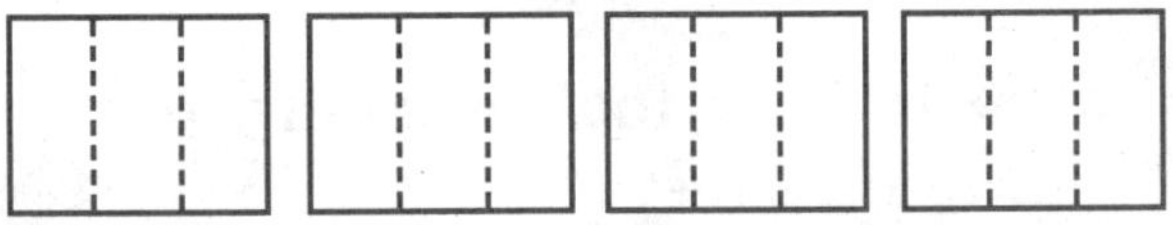

Step 3: Count how many groups of $\frac{2}{3}$ fit into the rectangles.

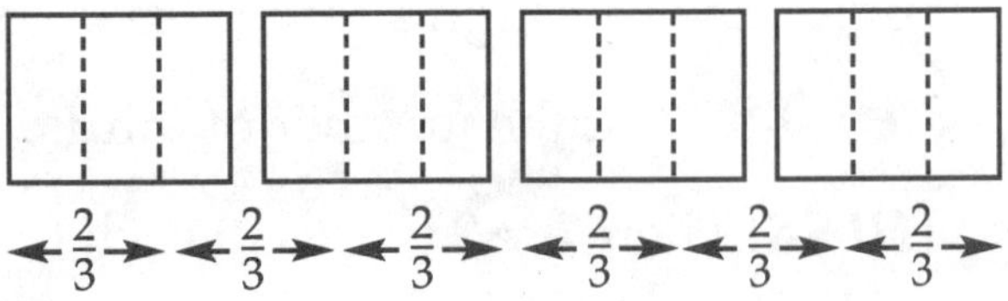

How many groups of $\frac{2}{3}$ fit? __6__ groups

So, Rita has __6__ servings of juice.

Name ________________

PRACTICE

Draw a model to help you solve each problem. Then solve.

3. **Dave uses $\frac{1}{2}$ cup of sugar when he makes 1 pitcher of iced tea. How many pitchers of iced tea can he make with 3 cups of sugar?**

Students' models will vary. Check that models represent the problems accurately.

He can make 6 pitchers of iced tea.

4. **Jed has 2 cups of applesauce. The dessert cups hold $\frac{2}{3}$ cup each. How many dessert cups can he fill with the applesauce?**

Jed can fill 3 dessert cups.

5. **Lisette has 9 yards of ribbon. She decides to cut the ribbon into strips $\frac{3}{4}$ of a yard long to make streamers for a party. How many streamers can she cut?**

Lisette can cut 12 streamers.

6. **Nina has a 5-lb bag of peanuts. She can fit $\frac{5}{8}$ lb into one plastic snack bag. How many snack bags can she fill with peanuts?**

Nina can fill 8 snack bags.

TEST-TAKING PRACTICE

Choose the best solution for each problem. In the answer section at the bottom of the page, fill in the box of your choice.

1. **A banner is 7 ft long. Lita is attaching stickers every $\frac{1}{3}$ ft. How many stickers does she need for the whole banner?** D

   A $\frac{3}{7}$ C 7
   B $2\frac{1}{3}$ D 21

2. **A track is 2 mi long. It has markers posted every $\frac{1}{4}$ mi. How many markers does it have?** L

   J 2 L 8
   K 4 M 10

3. **A thermos holds 6 c of liquid. The drinking cup holds $\frac{3}{4}$ c. How many times can the drinking cup be filled from the thermos?** C

   A 6 C 8
   B 7 D 9

4. **A recipe calls for $\frac{2}{3}$ c of raisins per serving. How many servings can Elena make if she has 4 c of raisins?** J

   J 6 L 9
   K 8 M 12

5. **Janus has 4 m of string. He must cut the string into $\frac{2}{5}$-m pieces for a science project. How many pieces can he cut?** B

   A 8 C 16
   B 10 D 20

Write About It

Write a plan for solving the following problem. Then solve.

6. **A truck holds 5 T of coal when full. If it delivers loads of $\frac{5}{6}$ T each, how many loads can a full truck deliver?**

   Draw 5 rectangles to show 5 tons.

   Divide the rectangles into sixths.

   Then count the number of groups of

   $\frac{5}{6}$ that fit into the rectangles.

   $5 \div \frac{5}{6} = 6$;

   The truck can deliver 6 loads.

1.	A ❑	B ❑	C ❑	D ☒
2.	J ❑	K ❑	L ☒	M ❑
3.	A ❑	B ❑	C ☒	D ❑
4.	J ☒	K ❑	L ❑	M ❑
5.	A ❑	B ☒	C ❑	D ❑

Name ____________________

Explaining the Problem in Your Own Words

Sometimes you can solve a problem more easily if you show the information in another way. Rewrite the problem in your own words as a word equation.

Example

Phil bought 6 blank cassette tapes.
The total cost was $21.
What was the cost of one blank tape?

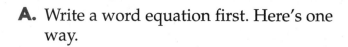

A. Write a word equation first. Here's one way.

Total cost ÷ Number of tapes = Cost of one tape

B. The word equation has three pieces of information.

Decide which information you know and which you don't know.

Number of tapes	⇒	6
Cost of one tape	⇒	don't know
Total cost	⇒	$21

C. Rewrite your word equation as a mathematical equation.

If you know a number, use it.

If you don't know a number, use a variable to show you want to find that number.

Total cost	÷	**Number of tapes**	=	**Cost of one tape**
↓		↓		↓
21	÷	6	=	n

D. Find the value of the variable.

$21 \div 6 = n$

$3.50 = n$

So, one tape cost $ 3.50 .

GUIDED PRACTICE

1. Will bought 3 T-shirts. Each T-shirt had the same price. The total price was $46.50. What was the price of each T-shirt?

   a. Write a word equation. Here's one way.

   Total price ÷ Number of shirts = Price of one shirt

   b. Write what you know and don't know. Then write a math equation by using that information and a word equation.

   Number of shirts ⇒ 3
   Price of one shirt ⇒ don't know
   Total price ⇒ $46.50

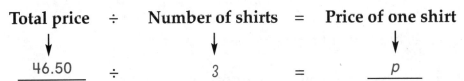

Total price	÷	**Number of shirts**	=	**Price of one shirt**
↓		↓		↓
46.50	÷	3	=	p

   c. Find the value of the variable.

   p = 15.50

   So, each shirt cost $ 15.50.

2. At the carnival, Latoya gave her sister half of the tickets she had. Latoya then had 18 tickets. How many tickets did Latoya have at first?

   a. Write a word equation.

   Total tickets ÷ 2 = Tickets Latoya has left.

   b. Write what you know and don't know. Then write a math equation by using that information and a variable.

   Number of tickets to sister ⇒ half the total
   Total tickets ⇒ don't know
   Tickets left ⇒ 18

   t ÷ 2 = 18

   c. Find the value of the variable.

   t = 36

   So, Latoya had 36 tickets at first.

Name ______________________

PRACTICE

Write a word equation for each problem. Write what you know and don't know. Then write a math equation that has a variable. Find the value of the variable to solve the problem.
Answers may vary. Sample answers are given.

3. **Maria has 140 books to pack in boxes. Each packing box can hold 20 books. How many boxes will she need?**

   140 books ÷ 20 books per box =

   Number of boxes

   $140 \div 20 = b$

   Maria will need 7 boxes.

4. **Otis is reading a book that has 275 pages. He has read 147 pages so far. How many more pages must he read to finish the book?**

   275 total pages − 147 pages read =

   Number of pages left

   $275 - 147 = n$ $128 = n$

   Otis must read 128 more pages.

5. **The swim team is washing cars to raise money for a trip. The trip will cost $350. The members will earn $5 for each car wash. How many cars must the members wash to raise all the money?**

   $350 total ÷ $5 per car =

   Number of cars

   $350 \div 5 = c$ $70 = c$

   The members must wash 70 cars.

6. **Ms. Lopez arranged her campers in groups of exactly 4 for a nature project. She was able to make 8 groups. How many campers does she have in all?**

   Groups of 4 x 8 groups =

   Number of campers

   $4 \times 8 = n$ $32 = n$

   Ms. Lopez has 32 campers.

7. **Jamal went to the movies with $15. When he came home, he had $2.50. How much did he spend at the movies?**

   $15 total − $2.50 = Amount spent

   $15 - 2.50 = m$

   $12.50 = m$

   Jamal spent $12.50.

8. **Luz, Rita, and Sue found a box of seashells in their grandmother's attic. The box held 72 shells. They decided to share them equally. How many shells did each girl get?**

   72 shells total ÷ 3 girls =

   Shells per girl

   $72 \div 3 = s$ $24 = s$

   Each girl got 24 shells.

TEST-TAKING PRACTICE

Choose the best equation for solving each problem. Fill in the answer box of your choice in the section at the bottom of the page.

1. **The library charges 5¢ per day for books that are late. Raul paid a fine of 35¢ for one book he returned. How many days late was the book?** B

   A $35 - d = 5$ C $d + 5 = 35$
   B $5 \times d = 35$ D $d \div 5 = 35$

2. **Tom can fit 8 video games in a shoe box. How many shoe boxes will he need if he has 40 games?** L

   J $b + 8 = 40$ L $8 \times b = 40$
   K $40 - b = 8$ M $b \div 8 = 40$

3. **Mrs. Ruiz is planning her flower garden. She wants to plant 96 tulip bulbs in 6 rows. How many bulbs should she plant in each row?** D

   A $96 + 6 = 102$ C $96 \times 6 = 576$
   B $96 - 6 + 90$ D $96 \div 6 = 16$

4. **Loretta earns $4.50 per hour to baby-sit children. Last Saturday she baby-sat for 5 hours. How much money did Loretta earn?** K

   J $4.50 + 5 = 4.55$
   K $4.50 \times 5 = 22.50$
   L $4.50 - 5 = 4.55$
   M $4.50 \div 5 = 0.90$

Solve each problem. Fill in the answer box of your choice in the section at the bottom of the page.

5. **Darryl gave half his baseball cards to his brother. He has 48 cards left. How many did he have before he gave some to his brother?** D

   A 24 cards C 46 cards
   B 100 cards D 96 cards

6. **Trini bought a CD at the mall. She gave the clerk $20 and got $7.45 in change. How much did the CD cost?** J

   J $12.55 L $5.12
   K $8.55 M $12.45

Write About It

Write a plan for solving this problem.

7. **Felicia bought 2 pens that were the same price and a notebook that cost $3. Her total bill was $5.50. What was the price of one pen?**

   Students should show that they can subtract $3 from the total cost and divide the difference by 2 to find the cost of one pen.

   $5.50 - 3 = 2.50$

   $2.50 \div 2 = 1.25$

1.	A ☐	B ☒	C ☐	D ☐	4.	J ☐	K ☒	L ☐	M ☐
2.	J ☐	K ☐	L ☒	M ☐	5.	A ☐	B ☐	C ☐	D ☒
3.	A ☐	B ☐	C ☐	D ☒	6.	J ☒	K ☐	L ☐	M ☐

Name ______________________________ **Chapter 8 L2**

Drawing a Number Line

Drawing a number line can help you solve problems that use positive and negative integers.

Example 1

When Jake woke up on Monday, the temperature was -8 degrees. By noon, the temperature had risen 6 degrees. What was the temperature at noon?

A. Decide how to solve the problem.

I should count up __6__ degrees from -8°C.

B. Draw a number line.

Mark the line with a dot to show -8°C.

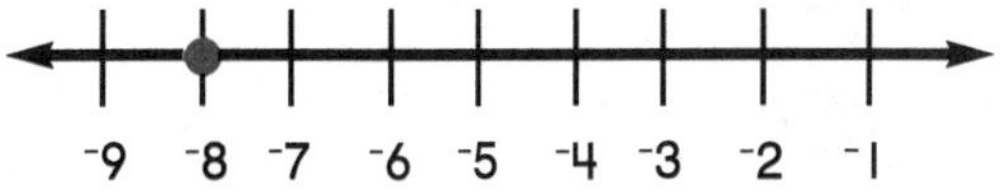

C. Use the number line to solve the problem.

Begin at the dot you have drawn, then move 6 places to the right.

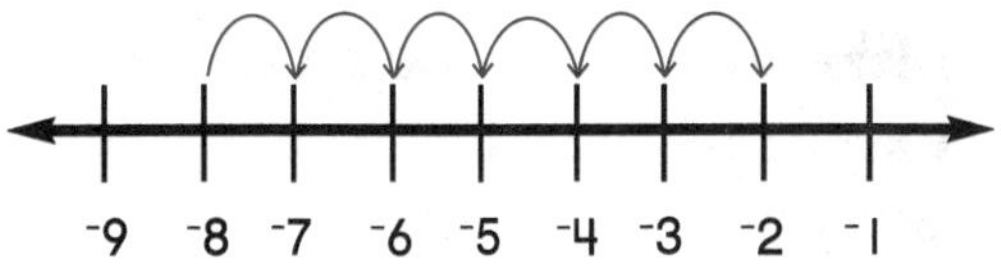

At which number do you end up? __-2__

So, the temperature at noon was __-2__ °C.

Example 2

On Tuesday morning, the temperature was -2°C. By noon, it had dropped 3 degrees. What was the temperature at noon?

Step 1: Decide how to solve the problem.

I should count down __3__ degrees from -2°C.

Step 2: Use a number line to solve the problem.

Mark the line with a dot to show -2°C, then move 3 places to the left.

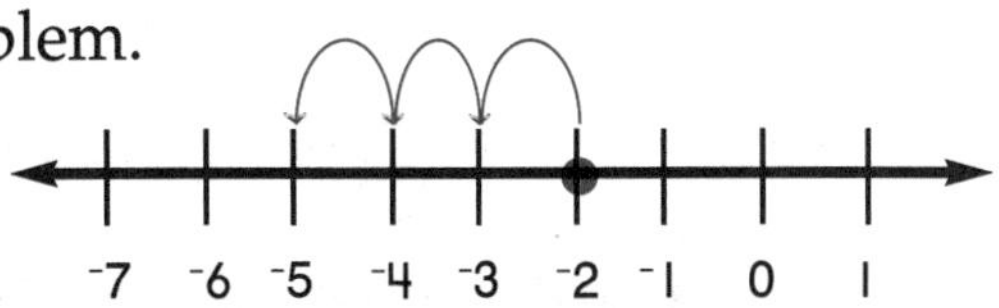

At which number do you end up? __-5__

So, the temperature at noon was __-5__ °C.

GUIDED PRACTICE

1. At noon, the thermometer read -4°C. At sunset, the temperature was -10°C. How many degrees had the temperature dropped?

   Step 1: Decide how to solve the problem.

   I should find the change from ___-4___ °C to ___-10___ °C.

   Step 2: Draw a number line.

   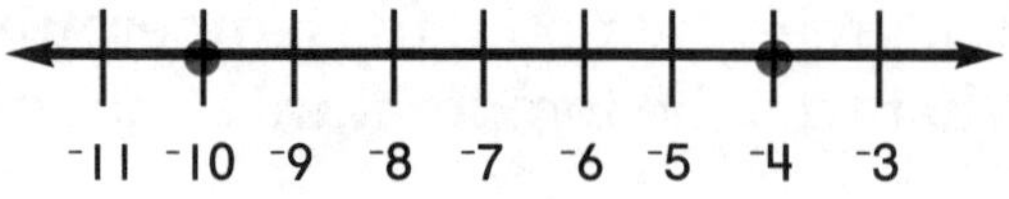

   Mark the line with dots to show -4°C and -10°C.

   Step 3: Use the number line to solve the problem.

   Count the spaces from -4°C to -10°C.

   There are ___6___ spaces. You need to count down (to the left).

   So, the temperature had dropped ___6___ degrees.

2. Mike measured the temperature of a liquid in a science experiment and found it was -1°C. He heated the liquid to a temperature of +3°C. By how many degrees did the temperature of the liquid change? Did it increase or decrease?

   Step 1: Decide how to solve the problem.

   I should find the change from ___-1___ °C to ___3___ °C.

   Step 2: Draw a number line.

   Mark the line with dots to show -1°C and +3°C.

   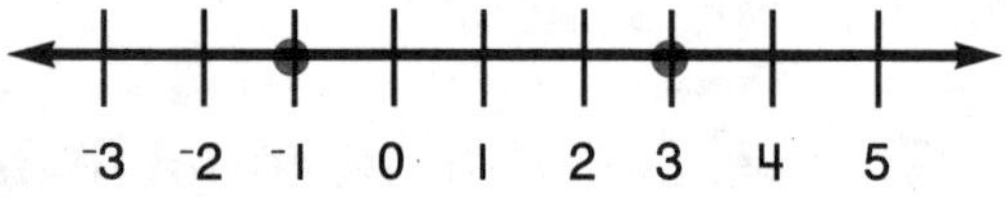

   Step 3: Use the number line to solve the problem.

   Count the spaces from -1°C to 3°C.

   There are ___4___ spaces. You need to count up (to the right).

   So, the temperature changed by ___4___ degrees.

   It ___increased___.

Name ______________________________ **Chapter 8** **L2**

PRACTICE

Mark the number lines to solve each problem.

3. How many degrees warmer is a temperature of $^{-}3$°C than a temperature of $^{-}8$°C?

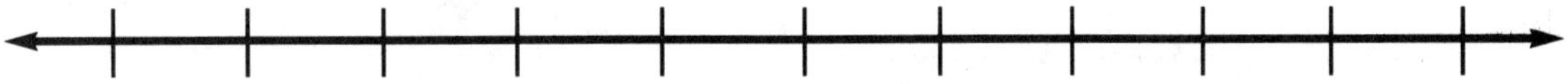

5 degrees warmer

4. The temperatures of two liquids in a science experiment are $^{-}6$°C and $^{+}1$°C. What is the difference between the two temperatures?

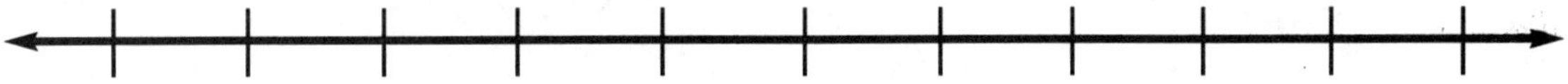

7 degrees

5. When Paul left for school it was $^{+}5$°C. During the afternoon the temperature dropped 7 degrees. What was the temperature when Paul came home from school?

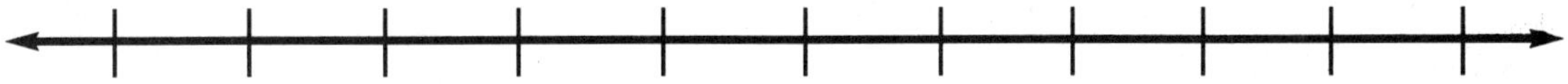

$^{-}2$°C

6. Sue's town is 7 degrees warmer than Bob's town, where the temperature is $^{-}16$°C. What is the temperature in Sue's town?

$^{-}9$°C

7. On Monday it was $^{-}10$°C. The temperature rose 12 degrees on Tuesday and then dropped 5 degrees on Wednesday. What was the temperature on Wednesday?

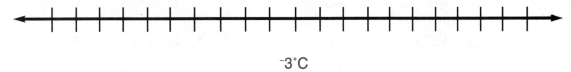

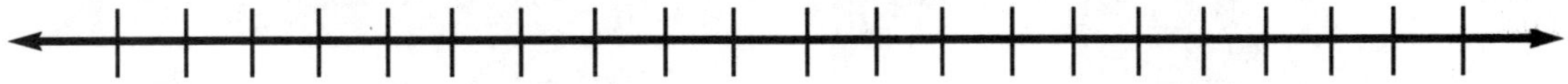

$^{-}3$°C

TEST-TAKING PRACTICE

Choose the best answer for each problem. Fill in the answer box of your choice in the section at the bottom of the page.

1. Which problem is shown on this number line? A

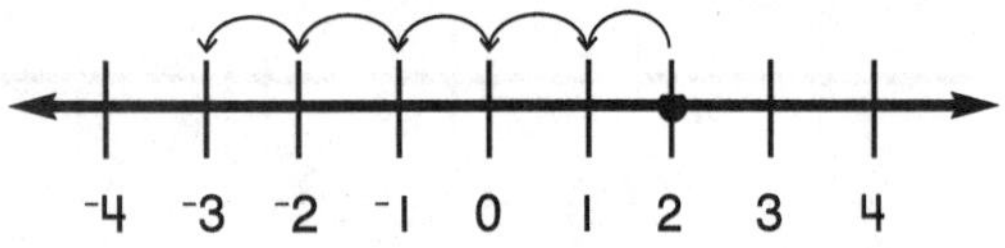

A $2 - 5 = n$ C $2 - 3 = n$
B $^-3 - 2 = n$ D $^-3 + 2 = n$

2. Which problem is shown on this number line? M

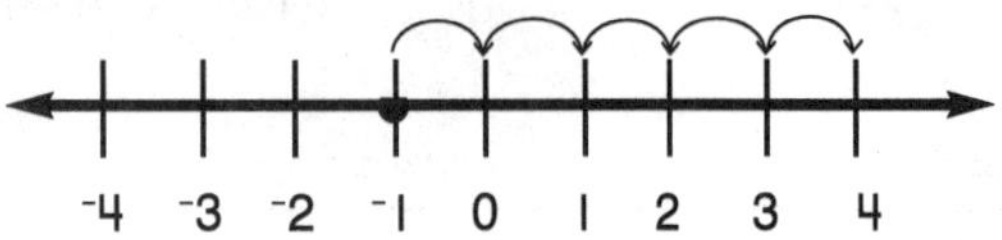

J $4 - 1 = n$ L $4 - {}^-1 = n$
K $^-1 - 4 = n$ M $^-1 + 5 = n$

3. Which problem is shown on this number line? B

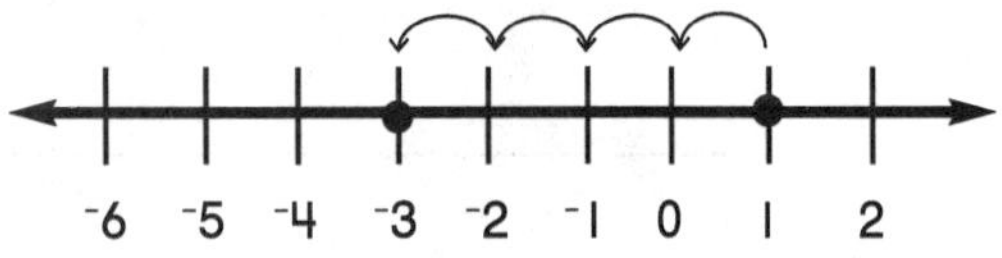

A $^-3 - 1 = n$ C $^-3 - 4 = n$
B $1 - 4 = n$ D $^-3 + 1 = n$

4. The temperature of a liquid was $^-3$°C. The temperature was increased by 10 degrees. What was the final temperature of the liquid? L

J $^-13$°C L 7°C
K 3°C M 13°C

5. The temperature at 6 A.M. was $^-12$°C. During the day, the temperature rose 8 degrees. What was the temperature at the end of the day? B

A $^-20$°C C 4°C
B $^-4$°C D 20°C

Write About It

Explain how you could use a number line to solve the following problem. Then solve.

6. The temperature at dawn was $^+3$°C. During the day, it dropped 7 degrees. What was the temperature at the end of the day?

Make a mark showing $^+3$ degrees on the number line. Then count 7 spaces to the left, and record the number.

$^+3 - 7 = {}^-4$

The temperature was $^-4$°C.

1. A ☒ B ☐ C ☐ D ☐
2. J ☐ K ☐ L ☐ M ☒
3. A ☐ B ☒ C ☐ D ☐
4. J ☐ K ☐ L ☒ M ☐
5. A ☐ B ☒ C ☐ D ☐

Name ______________________________ **Chapters 1–8**

Test-Taking Skill: Visualizing the Problem

If you have trouble understanding a problem, it can help to show the information in the problem a different way. Here are some ideas.

- Make a visual model, such as a diagram, a drawing, or a number line.
- Write a word equation or a number equation for the problem.
- Make a table to find a pattern.

Example 1

A swimming pool is 24 feet wide and 50 feet long. There is a row of blue tiles along each side. If there are 2 tiles every foot, how many tiles are there?

A 148 feet **B** 148 tiles **C** 296 feet **D** 296 tiles

THINK: Find the perimeter first, and then multiply by 2 to find the number of tiles. I can **make a diagram** to show the perimeter.

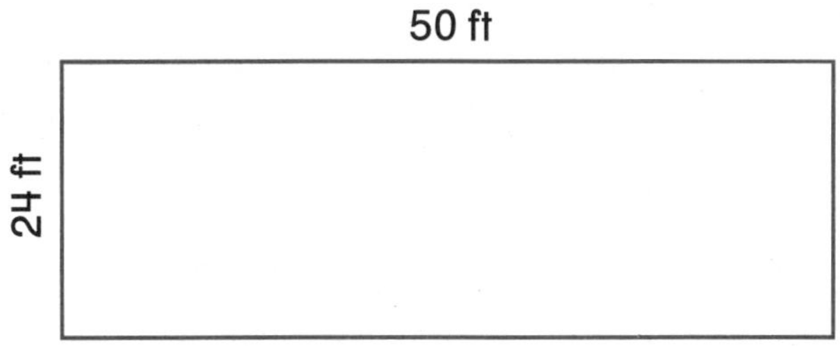

The perimeter is ___148___ ft, so the correct choice is ___D___.

Example 2

A pancake recipe calls for 1 quart of milk to make 24 pancakes. A camp cook wants to make 96 pancakes. How many quarts of milk does he need?

A 1 quart **B** 24 pancakes **C** 3 quarts **D** 4 quarts

THINK: I can **make a table** to find the number of quarts needed to make 96 pancakes.

Number of quarts of milk	1	2	3	4
Number of pancakes	24	48	72	96

The cook needs ___4 quarts___ of milk, so the correct choice is ___D___.

TEST-TAKING PRACTICE

Use the extra space on this page to show the problem in another way. Then solve the problem. In the answer section at the bottom of this page, fill in the box of your choice.

1. Lou planted 3 rows of vegetables. He planted beets 2 inches apart. He put the peas 5 inches apart. He left 8 inches between every two tomato plants. **At how many inches did all three rows line up?** D

   A 8 inches　　**C** 16 inches
   B 10 inches　　**D** 40 inches

2. The Radio Station has 982 CDs. They bought a CD rack with 8 sections. Each section holds 75 CDs. **How many CDs do not fit in the rack?** L

   J 75 CDs　　**L** 382 CDs
   K 300 CDs　　**M** 600 CDs

3. Masao walks to school and back home every day. The school is 4.7 kilometers from his house. **How many kilometers does he walk in 5 days?** D

   A 4.7 km　　**C** 23.5 km
   B 9.4 km　　**D** 47 km

4. Teo wants to buy a new coat that costs $79. He can earn $6.50 per hour baby-sitting. **How many hours will he need to baby-sit to buy the coat?** M

   J 5 hours　　**L** 12 hours
   K 10 hours　　**M** 13 hours

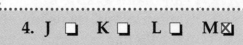

1. A ☐ B ☐ C ☐ D ☒　　**4.** J ☐ K ☐ L ☐ M ☒

2. J ☐ K ☐ L ☒ M ☐

3. A ☐ B ☐ C ☐ D ☒

Name ______________________

Writing Equal Ratios

You can solve some problems by showing information as a number sentence with two equal ratios. Using words may help you set up the two ratios so that their numerators and denominators match.

Example

Tracy drew this design for a sweater pattern. She used a scale of 3 mm on her drawing for every 10 mm on the actual sweater. In the drawing, the width of the *T* measures 27 millimeters. What is the actual width of the *T*?

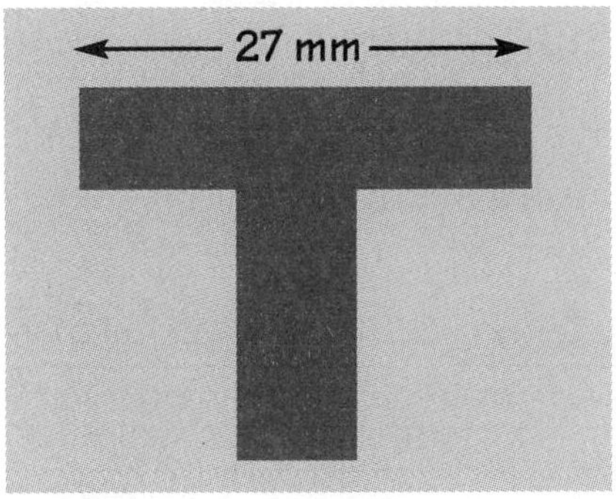

A. One of the ratios is the scale.

In words, describe the scale Tracy used.

In the drawing, __3__ mm stands for __10__ mm on the sweater.

B. Write the scale as a ratio.

$$\frac{\text{3 mm in the drawing}}{\text{10 mm on the sweater}}$$

C. Complete the number sentence. Write the second ratio so that the numerator and denominator match the first ratio. Use a symbol such as *w* for the unknown measurement.

$$\frac{3}{10} = \frac{\text{27 mm in drawing}}{w \text{ mm on sweater}}$$

D. Now, solve the number sentence.

$3 \times w = 10 \times 27$

$3 \times w = 270$

$w = 90$

So, the actual width of the *T* on the sweater is __90__ mm.

GUIDED PRACTICE

One centimeter on this map is equal to 5 kilometers actual distance on the ground.

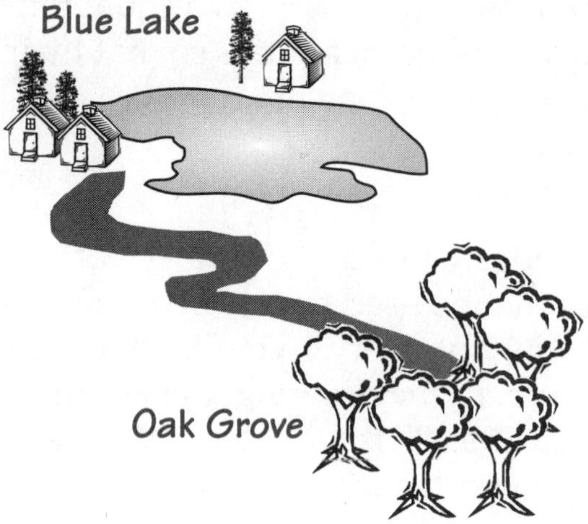

1. On the map, the distance from Oak Grove to Blue Lake is 3 centimeters. What is the actual distance?

   a. In this problem, the map unit is different from the actual unit.

   Write a word sentence to describe the map scale.

   On the map, 1 centimeter stands for
   5 kilometers actual distance
   on the ground.

   b. Write a ratio for the map scale.

   $$\frac{\text{on the map} \quad 1\ \text{cm}}{\text{actual distance} \quad 5\ \text{km}}$$

   c. Remember to match the first ratio when you write the second ratio. Choose a letter to represent the unknown number.

   Write a ratio for the distance between Oak Grove and Blue Lake.

   3 cm on the map / d km on the ground

   d. Use the two ratios to write a number sentence, or proportion. Then solve.

   $\frac{1}{5} = \frac{3\text{ cm}}{d\text{ km}}$; $d = 15$

   So, the actual distance between Blue Lake and Oak Grove is 15 km **.**

Name

PRACTICE

For problems 2 and 3, write a number sentence with equal ratios. Be sure the numerators and denominators match. Then solve the proportion to answer the question.

2. **Lauren can string 2 beads every 9 seconds. How many beads can she string in 45 seconds?**

   2 beads / 9 seconds, *b* beads/45 seconds, 2/9 = *b* /45, b = 10;

   Lauren can string 10 beads.

3. Nick is making a scale drawing of his garden. In his drawing, 1 centimeter stands for 4 meters on the ground.

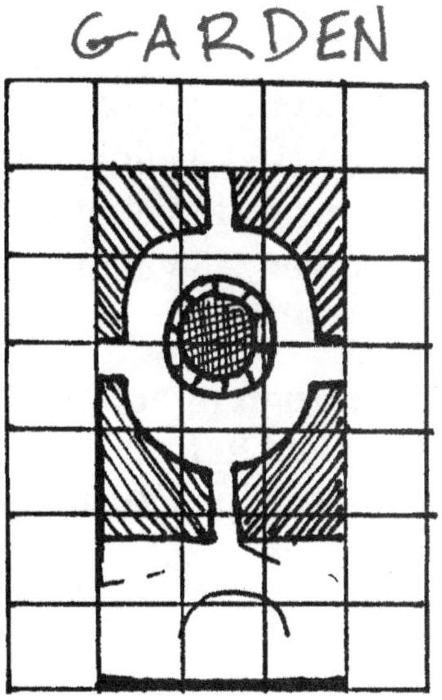

   a. **The garden is 28 meters long. What length will Nick draw the length of the garden?**

   1 cm/4 m, *l* cm/28 m, $\frac{1}{4} = \frac{l}{28}$, $l = 7$ cm

   b. **Nick drew a 3-cm line to show the width of the garden. How wide is the garden?**

   $\frac{1}{4} = \frac{3}{w}$, $w = 12$ m

Solve

4. Grapefruit are priced at 3 for $2. **How many grapefruit can you buy for $14?**

   21

5. On a map, 2 centimeters stands for 5 kilometers. The bicycle path Angie wants to take is 16 cm long on the map. **How long is the bicycle path?**

   40 kilometers

6. In basketball practice, Rashid shoots 3 foul shots every 40 seconds. **How many foul shots does he shoot in 120 seconds?**

   9

7. Rosalinda is on the volleyball team. On average, she serves 5 times every 3 games. **How many times does she serve in 15 games?**

   25

TEST-TAKING PRACTICE

Choose the best answer for each problem. In the answer section at the bottom of the page, fill in the box of your choice.

Use this problem for items 1–3.

Ruth is making yellow and green striped banners. She uses 7 green stripes for every 6 yellow stripes. How many yellow stripes does she need if she has 35 green stripes?

1. **Which ratio describes the proportion of stripes Ruth uses?** A

   A 7 green/6 yellow
   B 6 green/7 yellow
   C 7 green/13 yellow
   D 6 green/13 yellow

2. **Which pair of equal ratios can be solved to find the number of yellow stripes Ruth needs?** L

   J $\frac{6}{7} = \frac{35}{y}$ L $\frac{7}{6} = \frac{35}{y}$
   K $\frac{6}{35} = \frac{7}{y}$ M $\frac{y}{35} = \frac{7}{6}$

3. **How many yellow stripes does Ruth need if she has 35 green stripes?** D

   A 49 yellow stripes
   B 42 yellow stripes
   C 36 yellow stripes
   D 30 yellow stripes

4. **At a book fair, hardback books are priced at 3 for $5. Adam bought 18 books. How much money did Adam spend?** M

   J $15 K $18
   L $24 M $30

5. **On a map, 1 inch stands for 8 miles. The distance from Big River to Little River is 32 miles. How far is it between the two towns on the map?** B

   A 4 miles C 24 inches
   B 4 inches D 32 inches

Write About It

6. Explain how you would set up two equal ratios to solve this problem.

   Greg uses 9 quarts of water for every 1 sack of concrete mix. How many quarts of water will he need for 5 sacks of concrete?

   Possible answer: Write the ratio Greg uses: 9 quarts/ I sack. Use matching units and a letter or other symbol to write the second ratio: *c* quarts/5 sacks

1. A ☒ B ☐ C ☐ D ☐
2. J ☐ K ☐ L ☒ M ☐
3. A ☐ B ☐ C ☐ D ☒
4. J ☐ K ☐ L ☐ M ☒
5. A ☐ B ☒ C ☐ D ☐

Name ____________________

Making a Rate Table

In many problems, you are given a rate, such as dollars per hour or gallons per mile. A table can help you see the relationship between the two units that form a rate.

Example 1

One gallon of gasoline costs $1.32. Jonathan has $5. About how many gallons of gasoline can he buy?

Gallons	Cost
1	$1.32
2	$2.64
3	$3.96
4	$5.28
5	$6.60
6	$7.92
7	$9.24

A. Make a rate table by adding $1.32 again and again.

Look for a cost that is close to $5. Then read the number of gallons.

Exactly __4__ gallons of gasoline cost $5.28.

B. Reread the problem to be sure of the question you need to answer.

Jonathan can buy a little less than __4__ gallons of gasoline.

Example 2

Jonathan's car gets 25 miles per gallon of gasoline. About how many gallons of gas will he use on a 219-mile trip?

Step 1: **Complete the table.**

Gal	1	2	3	4	5	6	7	8	9	10
Miles	25	50	75	100	125	150	175	200	225	250

Step 2: **Look for the number of miles closest to 219. Estimate the number of gallons of gasoline needed for a 219-mile trip.**

Jonathan will use almost __9__ gallons of gasoline on a 219-mile trip.

GUIDED PRACTICE

Make and use tables to solve these problems.

1. Lian earns $18 an hour. About how long does it take her to earn $100?

   a. **Complete this table to show how much Lian earns for multiple hours of work.**

Hours	1	2	3	4	5	6	7	8
Earnings	$18	$36	$54	$72	$90	$108	$126	$144

   b. **Read the table. How much does Lian earn in an 8-hour workday?**

   Lian earns $144

   c. **Use the table to estimate. About how long does it take Lian to earn $100?**

   It takes Lian almost 6 hours to earn $100.

2. Hideo filled $1\frac{1}{2}$ baskets with cherries in the first hour. How long will it take him to fill 10 baskets?

   a. **Label each column in the table. Then complete the table.**

   b. **How many baskets can Hideo fill in 6 hours?**

   Hideo can fill 9 baskets in 6 hours.

   c. **Estimate how long will it take Hideo to fill 10 baskets.**

   It will take Hideo almost

   7 hours to fill 10 baskets.

Hours	Baskets
1	$1\frac{1}{2}$
2	3
3	$4\frac{1}{2}$
4	6
5	$7\frac{1}{2}$
6	9
7	$10\frac{1}{2}$

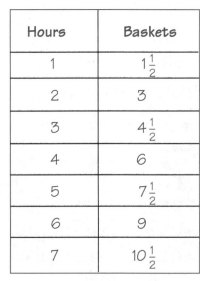

Name ____________________ **Chapter 9** **L2**

PRACTICE

For problems 3–6, use the outline provided to make a rate table. Use the table to solve the problems.

3. When he is at rest, Neil's heart beats 65 times each minute. How many times does his heart beat in 3 minutes?

   a. Fill in the table at the right.

   b. Solve.

   In 3 minutes, Neil's heart beats 195 **times.**

Minutes	Beats
1	65
2	130
3	195
4	260
5	325
6	390
7	455
8	520
9	585
10	650

4. **About how many minutes does it take Neil's heart to beat 500 times?**

   about 8 minutes

5. **Does Neil's heart beat more than 300 times or fewer than 300 times in 5 minutes?**

   more than 300 times

6. **Neil counted his heartbeats to estimate the length of a television commercial. His heart beat 265 times. About how long was the commercial?**

   The commercial was about 4 minutes long.

Solve

7. Willa's grocery bill last week was $57.83. **At $12 an hour, about how many hours did she have to work to pay for last week's groceries?**

   Willa had to work almost 5 hours to pay for the groceries.

8. Josh sells ice cream. There are 16 cones in one box. **If he sells 184 cones in a week, about how many boxes does he sell?**

   He sells about 12 boxes.

9. Rivka earns $6.75 an hour as a painter's assistant. **If a new tarp costs $40.00, how many hours will she have to work to buy it?**

   She will have to work 6 hours.

10. Elizabeth earns $12.25 an hour. **Does she earn enough in an 8-hour day to buy a coat that costs $89?**

   Yes

TEST-TAKING PRACTICE

Choose the best answer for each problem. In the answer section at the bottom of the page, fill in the box of your choice.

Lin's car can travel 22 miles on 1 gallon of gasoline. **Complete and use this rate table to answer questions 1–4.**

Gallons	Miles
1	22
2	44
3	66
4	88
5	110
6	132
7	154
8	176
9	198
10	220
11	242
12	264
13	286
14	308

1. Lin has 6 gallons of gasoline. How many miles can she drive? C

A 66 miles C 132 miles
B 120 miles D 220 miles

2. Lin drove 180 miles. About how many gallons of gas did she use? K

J about 4 gallons
K about 8 gallons
L about 10 gallons
M about 14 gallons

3. Lin's gas tank holds 14 gallons of gas. How far can Lin drive if she has a full tank of gas? D

A 22 miles C 220 miles
B 88 miles D 308 miles

4. Lin's 14-gallon gas tank is half full. If she drives 130 miles to visit her aunt, which statement is true? L

J Lin will run out of gas.
K Lin will have 5 gallons of gas left.
L Lin will not run out of gas.
M Lin's aunt will give her money for gas.

Write About It

Explain how you would set up a rate table and use it to solve this problem.

5. Jordan jogs 16 miles each week. Does he jog more or less than 80 miles a month?

Possible answer: Use the heads *Weeks*, *Miles*. Multiply to fill in the rate table. A month has less than 5 weeks. Find the point at which 80 miles is reached. He jogs less than 80 miles a month.

1. A ☐ B ☐ C ☒ D ☐
2. J ☐ K ☒ L ☐ M ☐
3. A ☐ B ☐ C ☐ D ☒
4. J ☐ K ☐ L ☒ M ☐

Name ______________________________

What Are the Units?

Answering a rate problem often means finding the *unit rate*. A *unit rate* compares units of one kind to a *single* unit of another kind: for example, miles per gallon or ticket sales per week.

Example

Beverly earned $104 in 4 hours. What was Beverly's rate of pay?

A. Find the unit rate to give the answer to the problem

Use the two kinds of units given in the problem to complete this sentence.

The unit rate is the number of ___dollars___ **for 1** ___hour___.

Write the unit rate as a ratio. Use *x* for the amount you do not know.

$$\frac{\underline{\ x\ }\ \textbf{dollars}}{\underline{\ 1\ }\ \textbf{hour}}$$

B. Use the numbers given in the problem to write an equal ratio. Match the numerators and the denominators to complete a proportion.

$$\frac{x\ \textbf{dollars}}{\textbf{1 hour}} = \frac{\textbf{104}\ \underline{\text{dollars}}}{\textbf{4}\ \underline{\text{hours}}}$$

C. Solve the proportion to find the unit rate. Then answer the question.

$x =$ ___26___

Beverly's rate of pay was ___$26 per hour___.

GUIDED PRACTICE

1. Joyce ate 75 grapes in 5 minutes. How many grapes did she eat per minute?

   a. Use the units in the problem. Complete this sentence.

   The unit rate is the number of ___grapes___ **for 1** ___minute___.

   b. Write the unit rate as a ratio.

   $\frac{x \text{ grapes}}{1 \text{ minute}}$

   c. Write the unit ratio and Joyce's eating ratio as a proportion.

   $\frac{x \text{ grapes}}{1 \text{ minute}} = \frac{75 \text{ grapes}}{5 \text{ minutes}}$

   d. Solve the proportion, and write a sentence to answer the question.

   How many grapes did Joyce eat per minute?

   $\frac{75}{5} = \frac{x}{1}$

   ___$x = 15$ Joyce ate 15 grapes per minute.___

2. Will drove 180 miles in 4 hours. At what rate did he drive?

   a. Complete this sentence:

   The unit rate is the number of ___miles___ **for** ___1 hour___.

   b. What is the ratio for the unit rate?

   $\frac{x \text{ miles}}{1 \text{ hour}}$

   c. In what units will the answer for this problem be expressed?

   ___miles per hour___

   d. Answer the question.

   Will drove at ___45 miles per hour___.

Name ______________________________

PRACTICE

For problems 3–6, complete the sentence about the unit rate. Then solve.

3. **Postcards are priced at 5 for $2.00. What is the unit price?**

   a. The unit rate is the number of dollars **for 1** postcard.

   b. The unit price is:

   $0.40 per postcard

4. **Sharon read 96 pages in 2 hours. At what rate did she read?**

   a. The unit rate is the number of pages **for 1** hour.

   b. The unit rate is:

   48 pages per hour

5. **Angela spent $735 on a 7-day vacation. What was her daily spending rate?**

   a. The unit rate is the number of dollars **for 1** day.

   b. The unit rate is:

   $105 per day

6. **Leroy spent $96 for 6 bouquets of flowers. What is the cost per unit?**

   a. The unit rate is the number of dollars **for 1** bouquet.

   b. The unit price is:

   $16 per bouquet

Solve

7. **Twelve muffins cost $5.40. What is the unit price?**

   $0.45 per muffin

8. **George built 15 models in 6 days. At what rate did he build the models?**

   2.5 models per day

9. **Karen wrapped 6 gifts in 30 minutes. At what rate did she wrap the gifts?**

   5 minutes per gift

10. **Ravi wrote 35 pages in 1 week. At what daily rate did he write?**

    5 pages per day

TEST-TAKING PRACTICE

Choose the best answer for each problem. In the answer section at the bottom of the page, fill in the box of your choice.

Use this problem for questions 1–3.

Ashraf walked 12 miles in 4 hours. At what rate did he walk?

1. **Which describes the unit rate?** A

   A The number of miles walked each hour
   B The number of hours for each mile
   C The number of hours per mile for each hour
   D The number of hours per week for each mile

2. **Which unit will be used to express the rate at which Ashraf walked?** M

   J miles **L** miles per walk
   K hours **M** miles per hour

3. **At what rate did Ashraf walk?** C

   A 3 hours
   B 3 miles
   C 3 miles per hour
   D 3 miles per walk

4. **Stuffed animals are priced at 2 for $4.98. What is the unit price for the stuffed animals?** M

   J $9.96 per stuffed animal
   K 4 per $9.96
   L 2.49 stuffed animals per dollar
   M $2.49 per stuffed animal

5. **Yolanda's long-distance call lasted 54 minutes and cost $6.48. What was the call's rate per minute?** B

   A $0.01 per minute
   B $0.12 per minute
   C 54 minutes per hour
   D $349.92

Write About It

Explain how you would figure out which units to use for the answer to this problem.

6. **Steven paid $9.72 for a box of 12 die-cast cars. What was the unit price of the cars?**

   Possible answer: The unit price is the number of dollars for 1 car. The ratio is dollars/car. The answer will be expressed in dollars per car.

1. A ☒ B ☐ C ☐ D ☐
2. J ☐ K ☐ L ☐ M ☒
3. A ☐ B ☐ C ☒ D ☐
4. J ☐ K ☐ L ☐ M ☒
5. A ☐ B ☒ C ☐ D ☐

Name ______________________

Drawing a Number-Line Segment

You can use a number-line segment to help you estimate a percent of a number.

Example 1

About 75% of the members of the drama club were at last night's show. The drama club has 84 members. About how many club members were at the show?

A. Draw a number-line segment. Above the segment, label the endpoints 0 and 84. Below the segment, label the endpoints 0% and 100%.

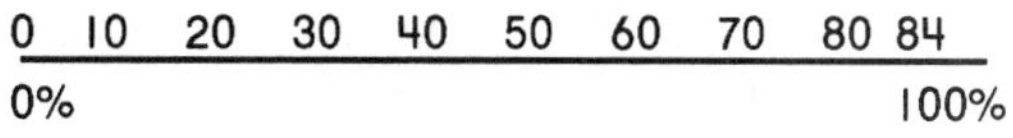

B. Think about the percents you know. Then write the percents below the number-line segment. First, write 50%. Then write 25% and 75%.

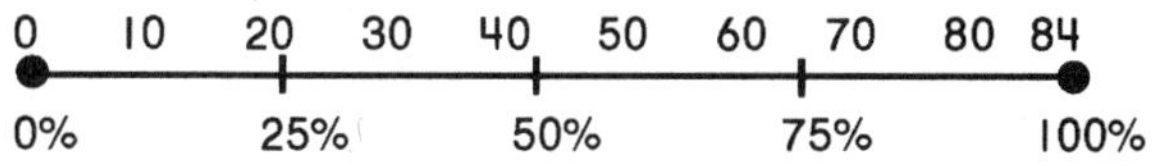

C. Use the model to estimate 75% of 84.

So, about 60 to 65 **club members were at the show.**

Example 2

About 20% of the members of the drama club were also members last year. Of the 84 members, about how many were members last year?

Step 1: Think about where 20% is located on the segment.

THINK: 20% is less than but close to 25%.

Step 2: Estimate the number that is above 20% on the number line.

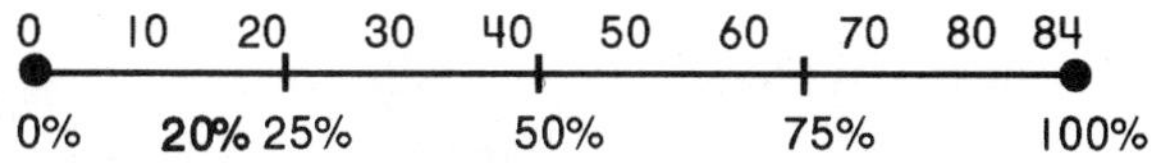

So, about 15 to 20 **members were in the club last year.**

GUIDED PRACTICE

You can use estimation to help you solve multiple-choice problems. Draw a percent model to help you solve the problems. Circle the correct answers.

1. Margie has a collection of 63 stuffed animals. She is planning to give 33% of them away. How many stuffed animals will she give away?

   A 21   C 42

   B 32   D 51

   a. Draw a number-line segment from 0 to 63. Below the line, label the endpoints 0% and 100%.

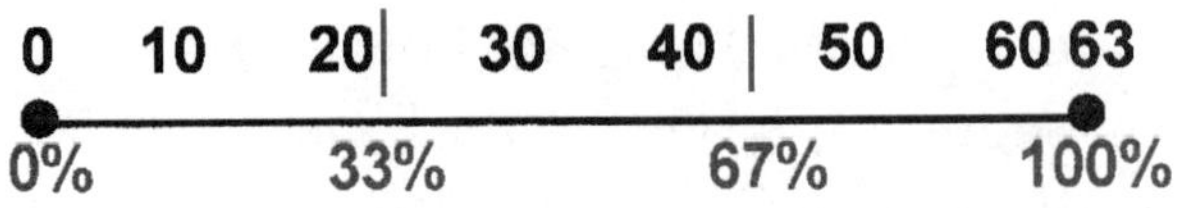

   b. Draw marks to show 33% and 67% ($\frac{1}{3}$ and $\frac{2}{3}$).

   c. Use the model to estimate 33% of 63. How many stuffed animals will Margie give away? A

   A 21   C 42

   B 32   D 51

2. Trevor works 40 hours each week. His work for this week is 50% done. How many hours has Trevor worked?

   J 5   L 20

   K 10   M 30

   a. Draw and label a number-line segment.

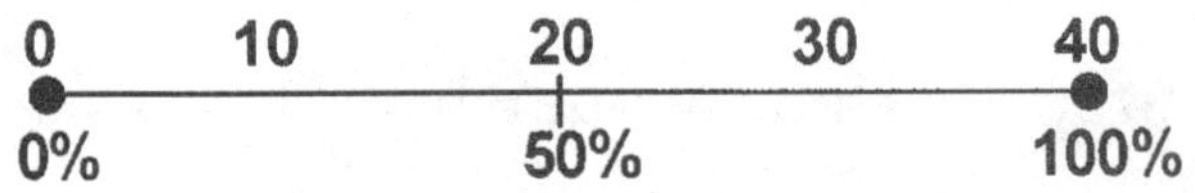

   b. Draw a mark to show 50%.

   c. Estimate 50% of 40 to answer the question. How many hours has Trevor worked? L

Name ____________________

PRACTICE

Use the space provided to draw percent models. Circle the correct answers.

3. There were 36 people on a train. At the South End Station, 25% of them left the train. **How many people left the train?** A

A 9 B 18 C 25 D 32

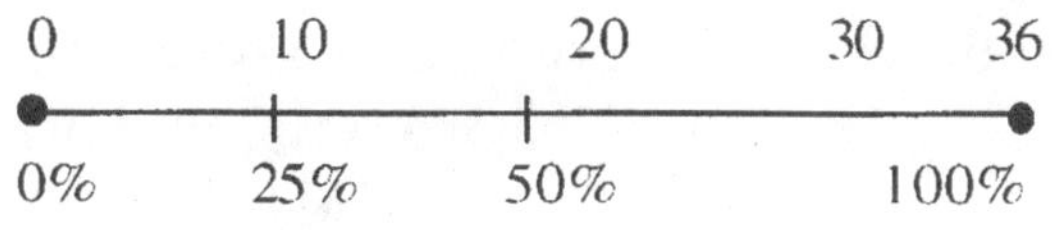

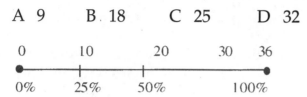

4. There are 50 bulbs in a package. Doris is going to plant 50% of them in her front flower bed. **How many bulbs will she plant in the front flower bed?** L

J 10 **K** 15 **L** 25 **M** 35

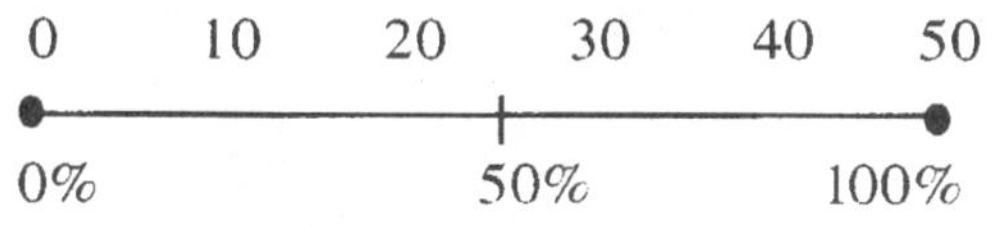

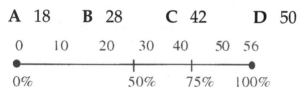

5. Of the 56 lights on Elm Street, 75% are working. **How many lights are working?** C

A 18 **B** 28 **C** 42 **D** 50

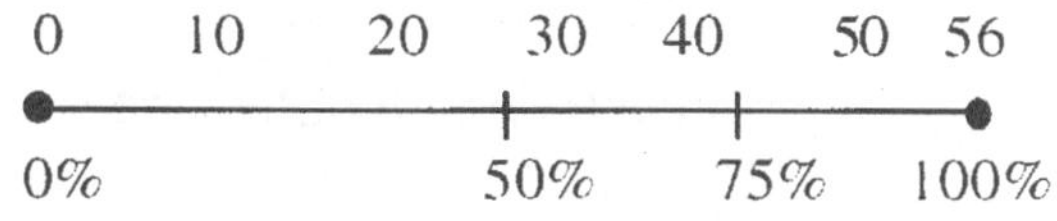

Estimate the answer.

6. David has the signatures of 42 major-league football players. His favorite team has 67% of those 42 players. **About how many signatures are by members of David's favorite team?**

about 20–30 signatures

7. Ms. Evans had $72 in her purse. She gave 25% of her money to her daughter. **About how much money did Ms. Evans give her daughter?**

about $15–$20

TEST-TAKING PRACTICE

For problems 1–6, choose the best answer for each problem. In the answer section at the bottom of the page, fill in the box of your choice.

1. **Mandy earned \$42. She wants to save 50% of her earnings. How much of the \$42 should she save?** B

   A \$7 C \$14
   B \$21 D \$35

2. **Hoshi needs 60 mg of vitamin C each day. He gets 25% of his vitamin C at breakfast. How many mg of vitamin C does he get at breakfast?** J

   J 15 mg L 25 mg
   K 40 mg M 52 mg

3. **Nina bought 27 sweatshirts for her store. Of the sweatshirts, 33% were size large. How many were size large?** C

   A 3 C 9
   B 18 D 21

4. **On a 44-question test Mark answered 75% of the questions correctly. How many questions did he answer correctly?** M

   J 8 L 15
   K 22 M 33

5. **Of 62 band members, 50% are marching in a parade. How many band members are marching?** C

   A 21 C 31
   B 41 D 51

6. **Pearl ordered 48 flowers. Of the flowers, 75% are daisies. How many are daisies?** M

   J 12 L 16
   K 27 M 36

Write About It

Explain how you could use a number-line segment to model this percent problem.

7. **Len tried 68 foul shots. He made 25% of them. About how many shots did Len make?**

   Possible answer: Draw a line segment. Label the endpoints 0% and 100% below the line and 0 and 68 above the line. Draw marks for 25%, 50%, and 75% to divide the segment into four equal intervals. Think of numbering the line in multiples of 10, and decide which number 75% is closest to.

1.	A ☐	B ☒	C ☐	D ☐	4.	J ☐	K ☐	L ☐	M ☒
2.	J ☒	K ☐	L ☐	M ☐	5.	A ☐	B ☐	C ☒	D ☐
3.	A ☐	B ☐	C ☒	D ☐	6.	J ☐	K ☐	L ☐	M ☒

Name ______________________________

Deciding How to Estimate

Sometimes, an estimate is all you need to answer a question. If you know that $\frac{1}{4} = 25\%$, $\frac{1}{2} = 50\%$, and $\frac{3}{4} = 75\%$, you can solve many percent problems by estimating.

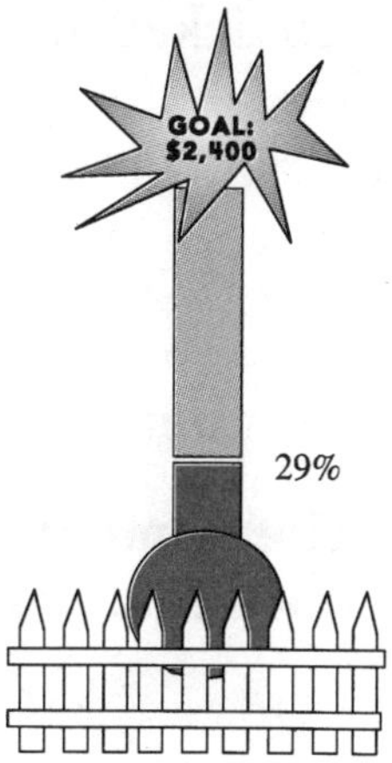

Example 1

The animal shelter needs $2,400 for new fencing. So far, it has achieved 29% of its goal. About how much money has it raised so far?

A. Use the fractions for 25%, 50%, and 75% as benchmarks.

29% is about 25%, or $\frac{1}{4}$.

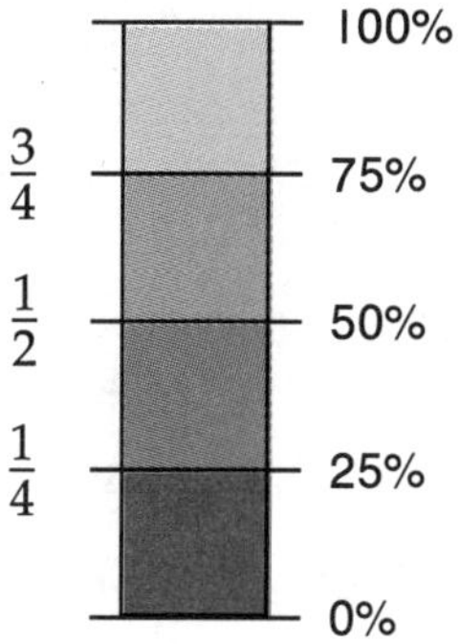

B. Find $\frac{1}{4}$ of $2,400 to estimate the amount of money raised so far.

$\frac{1}{4} \times 2{,}400 = 600$

C. Decide whether the amount the animal shelter has raised is greater than $600 or less than $600.

Because 25% is less than 29%, $600 is less than the amount of money raised so far.

D. About how much money has the animal shelter raised so far?

The animal shelter has raised a little more than $600 so far.

Example 2

The next month, the animal shelter raised $715. Has it raised 50% of the money it needs yet?

Step 1: Estimate 50% of $2,400.

$\frac{1}{2}$ of 2,400 = 1,200

Step 2: Calculate how much money has been raised.

$600 + $715 = $ 1,315

So, the shelter has **raised 50% of the money it needs.**

GUIDED PRACTICE

1. Of the 618 tickets sold for the matinee performance of *The Nutcracker*, about 46% were children's tickets. About how many children's tickets were sold?

   a. 46% is close to what fraction?

   46% is about 50 **%, or** $\frac{1}{2}$.

   b. The number of tickets sold was about 600. Find the fractional part of 600.

   $\frac{1}{2} \times 600 = 300$

   c. About how many children's tickets were sold?

   About 300 children's tickets were sold.

2. For an evening performance of *The Nutcracker*, 780 tickets were sold. About 78% of the tickets sold were adult tickets. About how many adult tickets were sold?

   a. What fraction can you use to estimate 78%? $\frac{3}{4}$

   b. Estimate the fractional part.

   $\frac{3}{4} \times 780$ is about $\frac{3}{4} \times 800$. $\frac{3}{4} \times 800 = 600$

   c. About how many adult tickets were sold?

   About 600 adult tickets were sold.

3. At the evening performance, 409 of the 1,189 seats were empty. Was the number of empty seats more or less than 25% of the seats?

   Estimate 25% of 1,189. About 300

   So, the number of empty seats was

   more **than 25% of the seats.**

Name ____________________

PRACTICE

Use the fractions for 25%, 50%, and 75%. Estimate to solve each problem.

4. Approximately 23% of the 156 people surveyed like Brand A chewing gum best. About how many people liked Brand A best?

$\frac{1}{4}$ x 160 = 40 About 40 people liked Brand A best.

5. There are 980 books to be sold at the library's book sale. About 55% of them are hardback books. About how many are hardback books?

$\frac{1}{2}$ x 1,000 = 500 About 500 are hardback books.

6. Eve spent \$156 on a dress and shoes. The dress cost 76% of the money. About how much did the dress cost?

$\frac{3}{4}$ x \$160 = \$120

The dress cost about \$120.

7. Of the 84 people taking a science class, about 77% plan to go on the field trip. About how many people plan to go on the trip?

$\frac{3}{4}$ x 80 = 60 About 60 people plan to go on the trip.

8. Mr. Mallory says that he spent 48% of his advertising budget on newspaper ads. If his advertising budget was \$640, about how much did he spend on advertising?

$\frac{1}{2}$ x 600 = 300 Mr. Mallory spent about \$300 on newspaper ads.

9. Mrs. Johnson spent \$278 to drive to Chicago. Gas cost 72% of the total.

a. Did she spend more than \$150 on gasoline?

Yes

Explain how you decided.

$\frac{3}{4}$ x 280 = 210. So, she must have spent more than \$150 on gasoline.

b. Did she spend more than \$200 on gasoline?

Hard to tell. $\frac{3}{4}$ x \$280 =\$210, which is very close to \$200.

TEST-TAKING PRACTICE

For problems 1–5, choose the best answer for each problem. In the answer section at the bottom of the page, fill in the box of your choice.

1. Brian scored 79% on his last test. About how many of the 120 items on the test did he answer correctly? C

A 65
B 80
C 95
D 105

2. Yolanda had $68 saved. She spent 44% of her savings on a gift for her mother. About how much did she spend for her mother's gift? K

J $20
K $30
L $40
M $50

3. Anton is saving for a $480 bicycle. So far, he has saved 19% of the amount he needs. About how many dollars has he saved? A

A $91
B $125
C $136
D $238

4. Of the 416 vehicles sold at Honest Hanna's last month, 28% were pick-up trucks. About how many pick-up trucks were sold last month? K

J 98
K 116
L 130
M 202

5. Shiro says that 53% of the stamps in his collection are from the United States. If he has 2,600 stamps, about how many are from the United States? C

A 650
B 1,222
C 1,378
D 1,550

Write About It

Explain how you would estimate the solution to this problem. Then solve.

6. In one week, 560 baskets of strawberries were picked at Strawberry Fields, and 73% of them were picked on the weekend. About how many baskets of strawberries were picked on the weekend?

Use the fact that 73% is about 75%, or $\frac{3}{4}$. Find $\frac{3}{4}$ of 560, or $\frac{3}{4}$ of 600. About 400 to 450 baskets were picked.

1.	A ☐	B ☐	C ☒	D ☐
2.	J ☐	K ☒	L ☐	M ☐
3.	A ☒	B ☐	C ☐	D ☐
4.	J ☐	K ☒	L ☐	M ☐
5.	A ☐	B ☐	C ☒	D ☐

Name ____________________

Writing a Word Equation

You can write a word equation to help you solve percent problems.

Example

Wayne budgets 5% of his earnings to buy clothes.
If he earned $720 this week, how many dollars does
Wayne budget for clothes?

A. Write a word equation that tells the whole amount, the part, and the percent.

Whole x Percent = Part

B. Rewrite the word equation with amounts from the problem.

Whole	x	**Percent**	=	**Part**
↓		↓		↓
Amount Wayne earns	x	5%	=	Amount for clothes

C. Replace the words with numbers.

Whole	x	**Percent**	=	**Part**
Amount Wayne earns	x	5%	=	Amount for clothes
↓		↓		↓
$ 720	x	**0.05**	=	n

D. Solve the equation, and answer the question.

720 x 0.05 = 36

So, Wayne budgets $ 36 **for clothes.**

GUIDED PRACTICE

1. Michelle ordered 300 bricks for a wall. So far, 225 bricks have been delivered. What percent of the bricks have been delivered?

   a. Write the word equation with amounts from the problem.

Whole	x	**Percent**	=	**Part**
↓		↓		↓
Bricks needed	x	n	=	**Bricks delivered**

   b. Replace the words with numbers.

Bricks needed	x	n	=	**Bricks delivered**
↓		↓		↓
300	x	n	=	225

   c. Solve the equation. $300 \times n = 225$

   Divide both sides by 300. $\frac{300}{300} \times n = \frac{225}{300}$ **So, n = 0.75, or 75%.**

   So, 75% of the bricks have been delivered.

2. Luke needs 70 bricks to make a planter. He has 20% of the bricks he needs. How many bricks does he have?

   a. Write the word equation with amounts from the problem.

Whole	x	**Percent**	=	**Part**
↓		↓		↓
Bricks needed	x	20%	=	**Bricks Luke has**

   b. Replace the words with numbers.

Bricks needed	x	20%	=	**Bricks Luke has**
↓		↓		↓
70	x	**0.20**	=	n

   c. Solve the equation. **70×0.20 =** 14

   So, Luke has 14 **bricks.**

Name ____________________

PRACTICE

Write an equation to solve each problem.

3. **Tina saves 15% of her earnings. She earned $640 last week. How many dollars will she put into savings?**

   640 x 15% = *n*

   She will put $96 into savings.

4. **Janice bought a video originally priced at $16 for 30% off. How much was the discount?**

   16 x 30% = *n*

   The discount was $4.80.

5. **A camera is regularly priced at $148. It is on sale for 25% off. By how much is the price reduced?**

   148 x 25% = *n*

   The price is reduced by $37.

6. **Doreen counted 36 cows in a field. Of the cows, 27 were standing. What percent of the cows were standing?**

   36 x *n* = 27

   75% of the cows were standing.

7. **There are 70 members of the Rose Society. At the last meeting, 28 members attended. What percent of the members attended?**

   70 x n = 28

   40% of the members attended.

8. **Leon took out a loan of $2,000. He paid the bank 10% interest on the amount he borrowed. How much interest did he pay?**

   2,000 x 10% = *n*

   He paid $200 interest.

9. **Of the $2,870 collected in a fund-raiser, 70% will pay for blankets for a homeless shelter. How many dollars will pay for blankets?**

   2,870 x 70% = *n*

   $2,009 will pay for blankets.

10. **Francine bought a new car for 95% of the sticker price. She paid $15,200 for the car. What was the sticker price?**

    n x 95% = 15,200

    The sticker price was $16,000.

TEST-TAKING PRACTICE

For problems 1–6, choose the best answer for each problem. In the answer section at the bottom of the page, fill in the box of your choice.

1. Sales tax is 6%. Which equation could you use to find the sales tax on a $16 book? C

A $16 ÷ 0.06 = sales tax
B sales tax = $16 + 0.06
C $16 x 0.06 = sales tax
D sales tax = $16 x 6

2. Julie has 72 videos. Of them, 18 are dramas. What percent of Julie's videos are dramas? K

J 18% L 45%
K 25% M 72%

3. Francis is saving for a $120 keyboard. She has saved 35% of the money she needs. How much money has she saved? B

A $35 C $55
B $42 D $76

4. A television is regularly priced at $450. It is on sale for 20% off. By how much is the price of the television reduced? M

J $360 L $180
K $240 M $90

5. Mr. Platt bought 144 calendars for his store. He has sold 108 of them. What percent of the calendars have been sold? C

A 108% C 75%
B 94% D 36%

6. Sales tax is 7%. How much is the sales tax on a dining room table that is priced at $300? J

J $21 L $210
K $37 M $307

Write About It

Explain how you could solve this problem, and then solve it.

7. A carton holds 25 boxes of cereal. In one carton, 19 of the boxes are damaged. What percent of the boxes are damaged?

Write a word equation, and then replace the words with numbers from the problem. Then solve the equation.

25 x n = 19; 76% are damaged.

1. A ☐ B ☐ C ☒ D ☐
2. J ☐ K ☒ L ☐ M ☐
3. A ☐ B ☒ C ☐ D ☐
4. J ☐ K ☐ L ☐ M ☒
5. A ☐ B ☐ C ☒ D ☐
6. J ☒ K ☐ L ☐ M ☐

Writing Word Equations

To solve problems with more than two steps, you can decide what to do first by making a list of the questions you need to answer.

In this example, you will need to use information from the advertisement at the right.

Example

Sarah gave the cashier $200 dollars for a CD changer that was on sale. How much change did she receive?

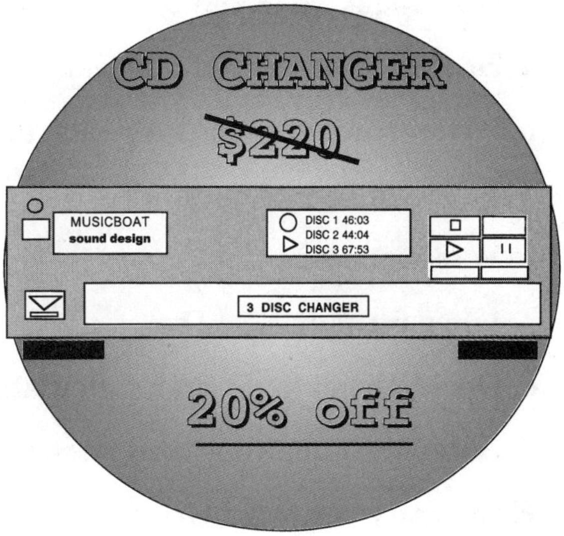

A. Make a list of the questions you need to answer.

- **How much change did she receive?**
- **How much did she pay?**
- **How much is 20% off?**

B. Write word equations for each question. Use numbers if you know them.

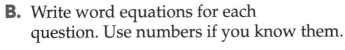

Change	=	**$200**	–	**Cost**
Paid	=	**$220**	–	**(20% off)**
20% off	=	**0.20**	x	**$220**

C. Decide which question is easiest to answer first.

THINK: **I know the numbers to calculate 20% off.**

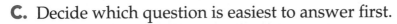

0.20 x $220 = $ 44

D. Use what you calculated to answer the other questions and solve the problem.

Paid	=	**$220**	–	$ 44	=	$ 176
Change	=	**$200**	–	$ 176	=	$ 24

So, Sarah received $ 24 in change.

GUIDED PRACTICE

The graph shows percentages of 200 votes. Greg carved entries C and D.

Pumpkin Contest Results

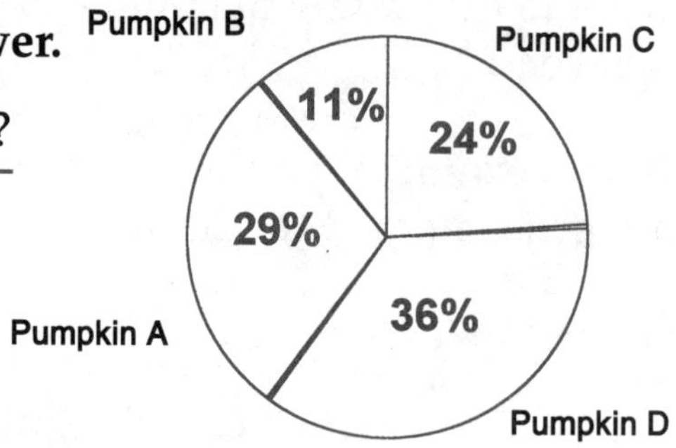

1. How many votes did Greg's pumpkins get?

a. Underline the questions you need to answer.

- How many votes did Greg's Pumpkins get?
- How many votes did pumpkin A get?
- How many votes did pumpkin C get?
- How many votes did pumpkin D get?

b. Write word equations for each amount that you need to find.

Votes for Greg's pumpkins = Votes for C **+** Votes for D

Votes for pumpkin C = 0.24 **x 200**

Votes for pumpkin D = 0.36 **x 200**

c. Decide what to do first. Calculate votes for C and D**.**

d. Solve the equations, and answer the question.

How many votes did Greg's pumpkins get? 120 votes

2. How many more votes did Greg's pumpkin D get than pumpkin A?

a. Write the questions you need to answer.

How many more votes did pumpkin D get than A? How many votes did pumpkin D get? How many votes did pumpkin A get?

b. Write word equations for each amount that you need to find.

Amount pumpkin D won by = Votes for D - Votes for A

Votes for D = 0.36 x 200 Votes for A = 0.29 x 200

c. Decide what to do first. Then finish solving the problem.

Votes for D = 0.36 x 200 → 72 Votes for A = 0.29 x 200 → 58

72 − 58 = 14

So, Greg's pumpkin D won by 14 **votes.**

PRACTICE

As you solve these problems, use what you know to decide which question to answer first.

3. If sales tax is 6%, what is the total cost of a CD player that costs $120 and a CD that costs $15?

   a. Underline the question that you will answer first.

   - How much are the two items without tax?
   - How much are the two items with tax?

   b. Solve the problem.

   Cost of both items without tax: 120 + 15 = $135

   Tax: 0.06 x 135 = $8.10 Total cost: $135 + $8.10 = $143.10

   So, the total cost for the 2 items is $ 143.10 **.**

Solve

4. Tony got 70% of the 20 problems right on his first math test. He got 19 out of 20 right on the second test. **How many more problems did he get right on the second test?**

   5

5. Marcia bought 2 CDs for $16.00 each and a tape for $8.00. The sales tax is 6%. **What was the total cost?**

   $42.40

Use the circle graph for problems 6–8. The graph shows percentages of 250 votes.

6. In an election, 250 club members voted. **By how many votes did Marquis win the election?**

   20

7. **In total, how many votes did Forrester and Cox get?**

   60

8. **How many more votes did Forrester get than Cox?**

   20

Election Results

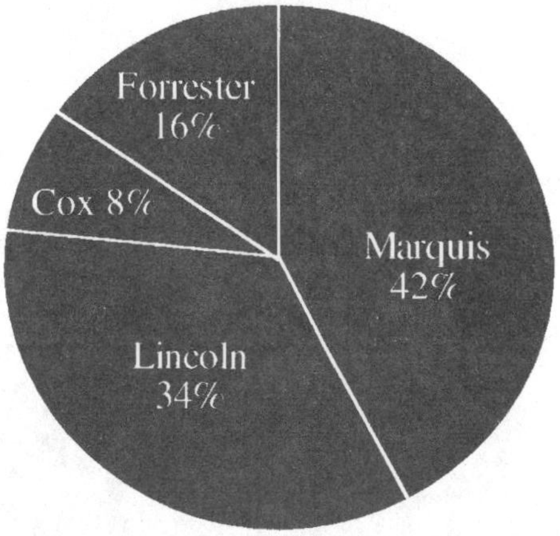

TEST-TAKING PRACTICE

For problems 1–5, choose the best answer for each problem. In the answer section at the bottom of the page, fill in the box of your choice.

1. Scott bought a shirt for $24. Sales tax was 6%. What was the total cost of the shirt? C

A $1.44
B $22.56
C $25.44
D $38.40

2. Nadia bought a fan for $30 and a radio for $90. The sales tax was 5%. What was the total cost? K

J $109
K $126
L $148
M $180

3. A model airplane regularly priced at $15.90 is on sale for 40% off. What is the sale price? D

A $6.36
B $7.95
C $8.75
D $9.54

4. At a 50%-off sale, Jackie bought items originally priced at $16 and $8.40. How much did Jackie spend? K

J $7.60
K $12.20
L $16.40
M $24.40

5. Of Audrey's note cards, 30% have animals on them, and 25% of the note cards have flowers on them. Audrey has 40 note cards. How many have either animals or flowers on them? D

A 2
B 18
C 20
D 22

Write About It

Explain how you would decide what to do first to solve this problem.

6. Robert had 80 baseball cards. He gave 25% of them to his sister. Then he bought 10 more. How many cards does Robert have now?

First, find how many cards Robert gave his sister by finding 25% of 80.

1. A ☐ B ☐ C ☒ D ☐
2. J ☐ K ☒ L ☐ M ☐
3. A ☐ B ☐ C ☐ D ☒
4. J ☐ K ☒ L ☐ M ☐
5. A ☐ B ☐ C ☐ D ☒

Name ____________________

Test-Taking Skill: Writing a Plan

On some tests, you need to explain how to solve a problem. It is important to explain your thinking and show your calculations.

Example

Keesha made trail mix. She began with $2\frac{1}{2}$ cups of oatmeal and added 2 cups of nuts, $1\frac{1}{2}$ cups of raisins, $2\frac{1}{4}$ cups of chocolate bits, $1\frac{3}{4}$ cups of sunflower seeds. She put the mix into 4 bags of equal size. How much mix did Keesha put into each bag?

A. Read the problem carefully. Decide on the kind of answer you need.

The answer is the amount of trail mix in each bag.

B. Write a plan for finding the answer.

First, I will add all the ingredients to find the total amount of mix.

Then, I will divide the total by 4 to find how many cups of trail mix Keesha put into each bag.

C. Solve the problem. Show your thinking and your calculations. Change your plan if you need to.

1: $2\frac{1}{2} + 2 + 1\frac{1}{2} + 2\frac{1}{4} + 1\frac{3}{4} = 10$

2: $10 \div 4 =$ $\underline{2\frac{1}{2}}$

D. Remember to answer the question in the problem.

Keesha put $\underline{2\frac{1}{2}}$ cups of mix into each bag.

TEST-TAKING PRACTICE

Write a plan to solve each problem. Explain your thinking.
Then solve.

1. Tara added $3\frac{1}{3}$ cups of flour and 2 cups of milk to the mixing bowl. Now, there are $7\frac{2}{3}$ cups of batter in the bowl. **How much batter was in the bowl before she added the flour?**

First, add the amounts of milk and flour. Then, subtract that from the total amount in the bowl to find how much batter was in the bowl before she added the milk and flour.

$3\frac{1}{3} + 2 = 5\frac{1}{3}$

$7\frac{2}{3} - 5\frac{1}{3} = 2\frac{1}{3}$

Before she added the milk and flour, the bowl held $2\frac{1}{3}$ cups of batter.

2. Sid weighed his puppy each week. At first, the puppy weighed $3\frac{1}{4}$ pounds. It gained $\frac{3}{4}$ of a pound every week for 3 weeks. The fourth week, it gained $1\frac{1}{4}$ pounds. **How much did the puppy weigh after four weeks?**

First, add the amounts the puppy gained for the 4 weeks. Then, add that amount to the puppy's original weight.

$\frac{3}{4} + \frac{3}{4} + \frac{3}{4} + 1\frac{1}{4} = 3\frac{1}{2}$

$3\frac{1}{4} + 3\frac{1}{2} = 6\frac{3}{4}$

After four weeks, the puppy weighed $6\frac{3}{4}$ pounds.

3. Leda has 5 scallop shells, 4 fan shells, and 7 oyster shells. **What fraction of her collection is fan shells?**

First, add the number of shells to find the total. Then, find what fractional part 4 is of that total.

$5 + 4 + 7 = 16.$ $4 \div 16 = \frac{1}{4}.$

Fan shells are $\frac{1}{4}$ of Leda's shell collection.

Name ____________________

Using Formulas

Sometimes, you must use a formula to solve a problem. Shown below are some formulas for finding perimeter (*P*) and area (*A*). The variables in a formula are often chosen so that the meaning of each letter is easy to remember. In these formulas, *l* stands for length, *w* stands for width, and *h* stands for height.

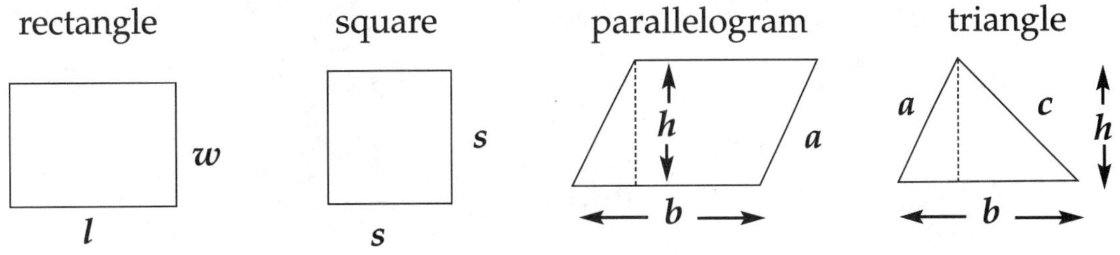

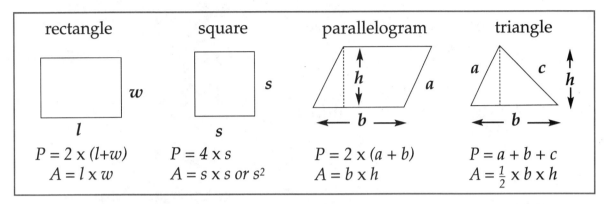

rectangle	square	parallelogram	triangle
$P = 2 \times (l+w)$	$P = 4 \times s$	$P = 2 \times (a + b)$	$P = a + b + c$
$A = l \times w$	$A = s \times s$ or s^2	$A = b \times h$	$A = \frac{1}{2} \times b \times h$

Example 1

Mr. Winston has a rectangular garden 20 ft long and 12 ft wide. How many feet of fencing will he need to completely surround the garden?

A. Decide which formula to use for the perimeter of a rectangle.

THINK: The length of the border of a figure is the perimeter.

P = __2 x (*l* + *w*)__

B. Substitute the values for *l* and *w* that are given in the problem, and solve.

P = 2 x (__20__ + __12__) so, *P* = 2 x (32) = 64

So, he will need __64__ ft of fencing.

Example 2

Each side of a square playground measures 20 m. What is the perimeter of the playground?

Step 1: Find the formula for the perimeter of a square. *P* = __4 x s__

Step 2: Substitute values for *s*, and solve. *P* = 4 x __20__ So, *P* = 80

So, the perimeter of the playground is __80__ m.

GUIDED PRACTICE

Use the table of formulas on the next page to solve these problems.

1. A triangular sail has a height of 14 ft and a base of 8 ft. What is the area of the sail?

Step 1: Find the formula for the area of a triangle.

$A =$ $\frac{1}{2} x b x h$

Step 2: Substitute the known values for *b* and *h*, and solve.

$A = \frac{1}{2}$ x 8 x 14

So, $A = 4 \times 14 =$ 56.

So, the sail has an area of 56 sq ft.

> Notice that area is measured in square units. Some units of area include square centimeters (cm²), square inches (in.²), and square feet (ft²).

2. A square photograph has sides measuring 8 in. How many square inches of glass would you need in a frame for the photo?

Step 1: Find the formula for the area of a square.

$A = s^2$ or s x s

Step 2: Substitute the known values for *s*, and solve.

$A =$ 8 x 8 So, $A = 64$.

So, you would need 64 square inches of glass.

PRACTICE

Use a formula from the table to solve each problem. Write down the formula you used and the solution.

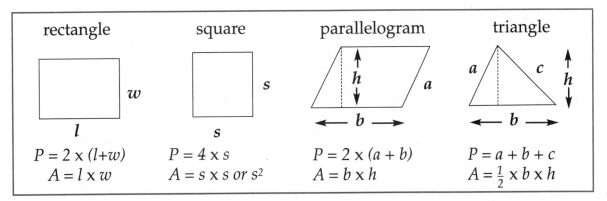

rectangle	square	parallelogram	triangle

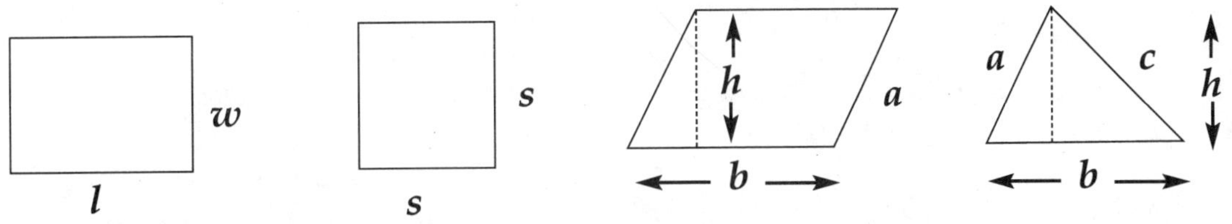

rectangle	square	parallelogram	triangle
$P = 2 \times (l + w)$	$P = 4 \times s$	$P = 2 \times (a + b)$	$P = a + b + c$
$A = l \times w$	$A = s \times s$ or s^2	$A = b \times h$	$A = \frac{1}{2} \times b \times h$

3. A triangular flag has a base of 4 ft and a height of 9 ft. What is the area of the flag?

$A = \frac{1}{2} \times b \times h$

$A = \frac{1}{2} \times 4 \times 9$ $A = 18$ sq ft

4. The sides of a square field measure 60 m. How many meters of fence are needed for the field?

$P = 4 \times s$

$P = 4 \times 60$ $P = 240$ m

5. A rectangular quilt measures 1.5 m by 2 m. How many meters of ribbon would be needed to sew around the border of the quilt?

$P = 2 \times (l + w)$

$P = 2 \times 3.5$ $P = 7$ m

6. A parallelogram has a height of 12 cm and a base of 20 cm. What is the area of the parallelogram?

$A = b \times h$

$A = 20 \times 12$ $A = 240$ sq cm

7. The sides of a triangular traffic island are 30 ft, 40, ft, and 42 ft. What is its perimeter?

$P = a + b + c$

$P = 30 + 40 + 42$ $P = 112$ ft

8. A rectangular wall is 9 ft high and 14 feet long. What is the area of the wall?

$A = l \times w$

$A = 14 \times 9$ $A = 126$ sq ft

TEST-TAKING PRACTICE

Choose the best solution for each problem. Fill in the box of your choice in the answer section at the bottom of this page. You can find the formulas in the table on the previous page.

1. A rectangular parking lot measures 40 yd by 30 yd. What is its perimeter? B

A 70 yd　**C** 210 yd
B 140 yd　**D** 1,200 yd

2. Will wants to know the area of his square garden so that he can decide how much fertilizer to use. The sides of the garden measure 15 ft. What is its area? M

J 30 ft　**L** 225 ft
K 60 ft　**M** 225 sq ft

3. The floor in a room measures 4 yd by 3 yd. Carpeting is sold by the square yard. How much carpeting will cover the floor? B

A 6 sq yd　**C** 14 sq yd
B 12 sq yd　**D** 24 sq yd

4. The sides of a triangular shawl measure 40 in., 65 in., and 40 in. How many inches of trim are needed for the border? L

J 40 in.　**L** 145 in.
K 105 in.　**M** 800 sq in.

Write About It

Write a plan for solving the following problem. Then solve.

5. A triangular road sign has a base measuring 15 in. Its height is 12 in. What is the area of the road sign?

First, find the formula for the area of a triangle. Substitute the known values in the equation and solve. $A = \frac{1}{2} \times b \times h$

$A = \frac{1}{2} \times 15 \times 12$; $A = 90$

The area is 90 sq in.

1. A ☐ B ☒ C ☐ D ☐
2. J ☐ K ☐ L ☐ M ☒
3. A ☐ B ☒ C ☐ D ☐
4. J ☐ K ☐ L ☒ M ☐

Name ______________________________

Drawing Examples

Some problems will ask you to decide whether a statement about a geometrical figure is true or not. Drawing examples of the figure can help you reach the correct answer.

Example

Is this statement true or false?

<u>A quadrilateral always has two diagonals</u>.

A. Try to draw a figure to support the statement.
A quadrilateral has 4 sides.
Draw a regular quadrilateral—a square.

THINK: A diagonal connects opposite vertices.
Draw diagonals in the square.
How many diagonals did you draw? ___2___

B. Try to draw a figure that does not support the statement.

Draw some more quadrilaterals, and construct their diagonals.
Try to draw a quadrilateral that does not have two diagonals.

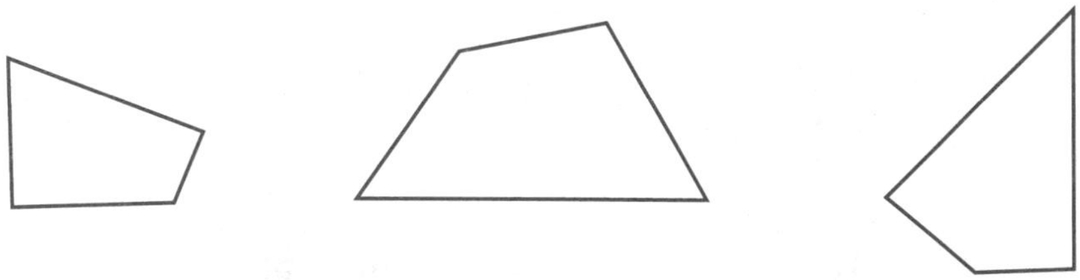

C. Refer to the figures you drew.

Could you draw a quadrilateral that doesn't have 2 diagonals?

___No___

Is the statement true or false? ___True___

GUIDED PRACTICE

1. Is the following statement *sometimes true, always true,* or *never true*? Intersecting lines are perpendicular.

   Step 1: Try to draw a figure that supports the statement.
   Draw two intersecting lines that are perpendicular.
   THINK: Lines that are perpendicular form a right angle.

   Can you draw intersecting lines that are perpendicular? Yes

   Step 2: Try to draw a figure that doesn't support the statement.
   Draw two intersecting lines that are not perpendicular.

   Can you draw intersecting lines that are not perpendicular? Yes

   Step 3: Refer to the figures you drew.
   Is the statement *sometimes true, always true,* or *never true*?

   Sometimes true

2. Is the following statement *sometimes true, always true,* or *never true*? A triangle has 2 right angles.

   Step 1: Try to draw a figure that supports the statement.
   Draw the base of a triangle. Draw a right angle at each end.

   Can you draw a triangle with 2 right angles? No

   Step 2: Refer to the figures you drew.
   Is the statement *sometimes true, always true,* or *never true*?

   Never true

Name ______________________

PRACTICE

Draw examples to help you decide whether each statement is *true* or *false*.

3. **A quadrilateral with 3 right angles is a rectangle.**

True

4. **Two of the sides of a triangle can be parallel.**

False

5. **A triangle has one diagonal.**

False

6. **A right triangle can have three congruent sides.**

False

Decide whether each statement is *sometimes true, always true,* or *never true.*

7. **A quadrilateral with four congruent sides is a square.**

Sometimes true

8. **A triangle with an obtuse angle is a right triangle.**

Never true

9. **A square has four right angles.**

Always true

10. **An isosceles triangle has two right angles.**

Never true

TEST-TAKING PRACTICE

Choose the best solution for each problem. In the answer section at the bottom of this page, fill in the box of your choice.

1. **If a quadrilateral has four congruent sides, it has four congruent angles.** B
   - A Always True
   - B Sometimes True
   - C Never True

2. **A quadrilateral with four unequal sides is a parallelogram.** L
   - J Always True
   - K Sometimes True
   - L Never True

3. **A quadrilateral with two right angles is a rectangle.** B
   - A Always True
   - B Sometimes True
   - C Never True

4. **If a triangle has three congruent angles, it has three congruent sides.** J
   - J Always True
   - K Sometimes True
   - L Never True

5. **A quadrilateral with four right angles is a parallelogram.** A
   - A Always True
   - B Sometimes True
   - C Never True

6. **A right triangle is an isosceles triangle.** K
   - J Always True
   - K Sometimes True
   - L Never True

Write About It

Explain how you could draw examples to decide whether the following statement is true or false.

7. **A triangle with no congruent sides cannot be a right triangle.**

Sample answer: Draw the base of a triangle, and draw a right angle at one end. Make sure that the side is not congruent to the base. Then construct and measure the third side. Use the figure to determine that the statement is false.

1. A ❑	B ☒	C ❑		4. J ☒	K ❑	L ❑
2. J ❑	K ❑	L ☒		5. A ☒	B ❑	C ❑
3. A ❑	B ☒	C ❑		6. J ❑	K ☒	L ❑

Making a Table to Show Possible Outcomes

For some problems, you need to find all the ways that two events could turn out. You can show the possible outcomes for two events in a table.

Example

This table shows the possible outcomes for spinning the two spinners.

Spinner 2

Spinner 1		1	2	3	4	5
	A	(A, 1)	(A, 2)	(A, 3)	(A, 4)	(A, 5)
	B	(B, 1)	(B, 2)	(B, 3)	(B, 4)	(B, 5)
	C	(C, 1)	(C, 2)	(C, 3)	(C, 4)	(C, 5)
	D	(D, 1)	(D, 2)	(D, 3)	(D, 4)	(D, 5)
	E	(E, 1)	(E, 2)	(E, 3)	(E, 4)	(E, 5)
	F	(F, 1)	(F, 2)	(F, 3)	(F, 4)	(F, 5)

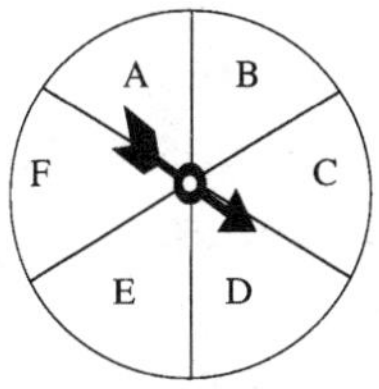

A. The outcomes for the numbered spinner are column labels in the table.

What are the column labels? 1,2,3,4,5

The outcomes for the lettered spinner are row labels in the table.

What are the row labels? A,B,C,D,E,F

B. At the intersection of each row and column is a letter-number pair called an ordered pair that shows a result of spinning the two spinners. Each ordered pair is written the same way.

What is the ordered pair for the result displayed on the spinners? (D,3)

C. How are the outcomes the same in row D? Each has a D.

How are they different? The numbers differ.

How are the outcomes the same in column 3? Each has a 3.

How are they different? The letters differ.

D. The table shows all of the outcomes possible if you spin the two spinners.

How many outcomes are there in the table? 30

So, there are 30 **possible outcomes.**

GUIDED PRACTICE

Bonnie has red, black, blue, green, yellow, and brown collars for her dog. She has red, black, and blue leashes. Make a table to show the possible collar-and-leash choices that Bonnie can make.

1. **Label the rows with the collar colors.**

   Label the columns with the leash colors.

2. **Complete the table. Write the collar-leash outcomes.**

	Red	Black	Blue
Red	(Red, Red)	(Red, Black)	(Red, Blue)
Black	(Black, Red)	(Black, Black)	(Black, Blue)
Blue	(Blue, Red)	(Blue, Black)	(Blue, Blue)
Green	(Green, Red)	(Green, Black)	(Green, Blue)
Yellow	(Yellow, Red)	(Yellow, Black)	(Yellow, Blue)
Brown	(Brown, Red)	(Brown, Black)	(Brown, Blue)

3. **How many collar-leash outcomes are possible?** 18
4. **In how many outcomes are the collar and leash the same color?** 3
5. **Can Bonnie use a green leash with a red collar?** No

Make a table to show all the possible outcomes if you draw one item from each of these bags.

6. **Label the rows and columns.**
7. **Complete the table to show the outcomes for drawing one item from each bag.**

	apple	peach	pear
circle	(circle, apple)	(circle, peach)	(circle, pear)
square	(square, apple)	(square, peach)	(square, pear)
star	(star, apple)	(star, peach)	(star, pear)

8. **How many possible outcomes are there?** 9

Name ______________________________ **Chapter 12** **L1**

PRACTICE

Make a table to show the possible outcomes for each pair of events.

9. **Suppose you spin the STAR and NUMBER spinners. In how many of the possible outcomes are both letters vowels (*a, e, i, o,* or *u*)?**

___2___

	N	U	M	B	E	R
S	(S, N)	(S, U)	(S, M)	(S, B)	(S, E)	(S, R)
T	(T, N)	(T, U)	(T, M)	(T, B)	(T, E)	(T, R)
A	(A, N)	(A, U)	(A,M)	(A, B)	(A, E)	(A, R)
R	(R, N)	(R, U)	(R, M)	(R, B)	(R, E)	(R, R)

10. **In how many outcomes is at least one letter a vowel?** ___12___

11. **Suppose a name is drawn from each hat below. In how many of the possible outcomes is one name a boy and the other a girl? (In this case, Alex is a boy.)** ___8___

	Ann	Alex	Sally	Ben
Bob	(Bob, Ann)	(Bob, Alex)	(Bob, Sally)	(Bob, Ben)
Mary	(Mary, Ann)	(Mary, Alex)	(Mary, Sally)	(Mary, Ben)
Roy	(Roy, Ann)	(Roy, Alex)	(Roy, Sally)	(Roy, Ben)
Kay	(Kay, Ann)	(Kay, Alex)	(Kay, Sally)	(Kay, Ben)

12. **In how many outcomes are both of the names girls' names?** ___4___

13. **In how many outcomes is at least one name a boy's name?** ___12___

TEST-TAKING PRACTICE

Choose the best answer for each problem. In the answer section at the bottom of this page, fill in the box of your choice.

For problems 1–4, suppose you take a card from each group.

1. **How many outcomes are possible?** C

   A 5 **C** 25
   B 10 **D** 50

2. **In how many outcomes do both cards show animals?** K

   J 2 **L** 6
   K 4 **M** 8

3. **In how many outcomes is at least one of the cards a flower?** C

   A 1 **C** 9
   B 5 **D** 10

4. **In how many outcomes is one card an animal and the other a flower?** K

   J 2 **L** 6
   K 4 **M** 8

5. **If you have three colors of shoes and 4 colors of socks, how many possible shoe-sock outcomes are there?** C

   A 6 **C** 12
   B 7 **D** 24

Write About It

6. **Suppose you can choose from red, yellow, or green socks. You can also choose boots, sneakers, sandals, or slippers. Explain how you would set up a table to find all of the possible sock-shoe outcomes.**

Possible answer: Label the rows of the table with the sock colors, red, green, and yellow. Label the columns with the shoe types, boots, sneakers, sandals, slippers. Complete the table by writing sock-shoe pairs.

1. A ☐ B ☐ C ☒ D ☐
2. J ☐ K ☒ L ☐ M ☐
3. A ☐ B ☐ C ☒ D ☐
4. J ☐ K ☒ L ☐ M ☐
5. A ☐ B ☐ C ☒ D ☐

Name ____________________ **Chapter 12** | **L2**

Making a Tree Diagram

Sometimes you need to find all the ways that three or more events could turn out. For these problems, a tree diagram is more helpful than a table for seeing all the possibilities.

Example

Suppose you flip a dime, a nickel, and a penny. In how many of the possible outcomes does at least one coin show tails?

A. The first event is flipping a dime.

The possible outcomes are heads and tails.

Write the event and the possible outcomes.

Dime
H
T

B. The second event is flipping a nickel.

For both dime outcomes, draw a branch to show heads and tails for the nickel.

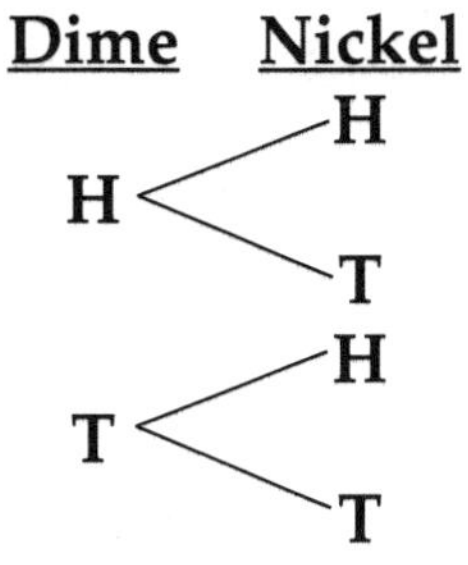

What are the possible outcomes if you flip a dime and a nickel?

(H, H); (H, T); (T, H) **;** (T, T)

C. Continue the tree diagram to show the possible outcomes for flipping a penny. Then write the outcomes for all three coins.

Complete the list of outcomes.

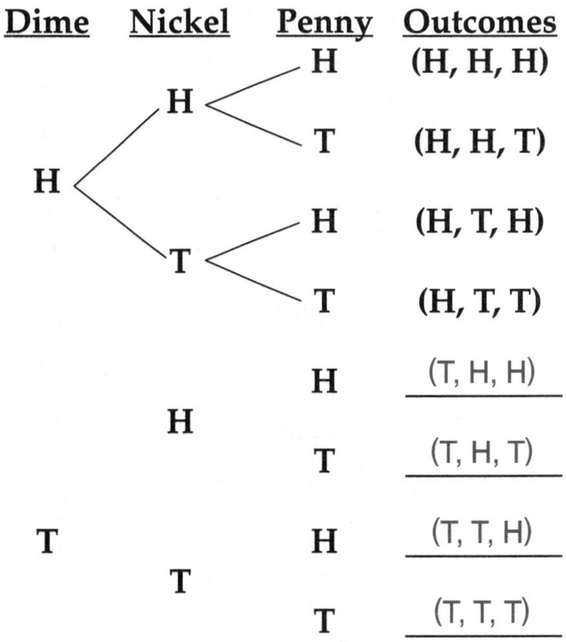

D. How many possible outcomes are there for flipping 3 coins?

8

E. In how many outcomes is there at least one tails result?

7

GUIDED PRACTICE

Suppose you spin each of these spinners. In how many of the possible outcomes do exactly two spinners show red?

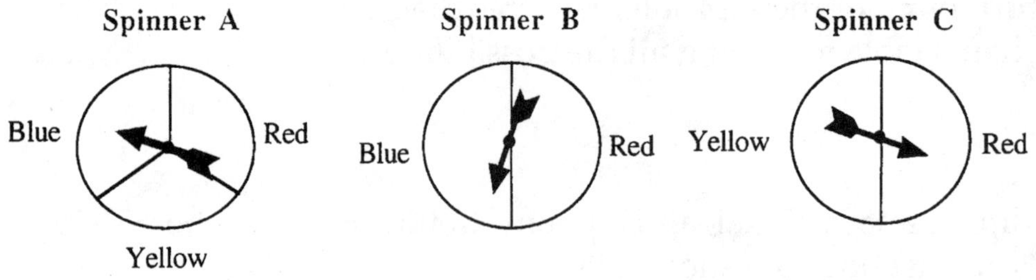

1. **What are the possible outcomes for spinner A? Complete the list of them in the tree diagram.**

Spinner A	Spinner B	Spinner C	Possible Outcomes
Red	Red	Red	(Red, Red, Red)
		Yellow	(Red, Red, Yellow)
	Blue	Red	(Red, Blue, Red)
		Yellow	(Red, Blue, Yellow)
Yellow	Red	Red	(Yellow, Red, Red)
		Yellow	(Yellow, Red, Yellow)
	Blue	Red	(Yellow, Blue, Red)
		Yellow	(Yellow, Blue, Yellow)
Blue	Red	Red	(Blue, Red, Red)
		Yellow	(Blue, Red, Yellow)
	Blue	Red	(Blue, Blue, Red)
		Yellow	(Blue, Blue, Yellow)

2. **What are the possible outcomes for spinner B? Complete the branches to match the outcomes for spinner A with each of the outcomes for spinner B.**

3. **What are the possible outcomes for spinner C? Complete the branches to include the outcomes for Spinner C.**

4. **Follow each branch of the tree diagram. Complete the list of possible outcomes for spinning the three spinners.**

5. **How many possible outcomes are there for spinning the three spinners?**

12

6. **In how many of the possible outcomes do exactly two of the spinners show red?** 4

Name ______________________________

PRACTICE

Suppose you draw a ball from each bag.

7. **Make a tree diagram to show all of the possible outcomes.**

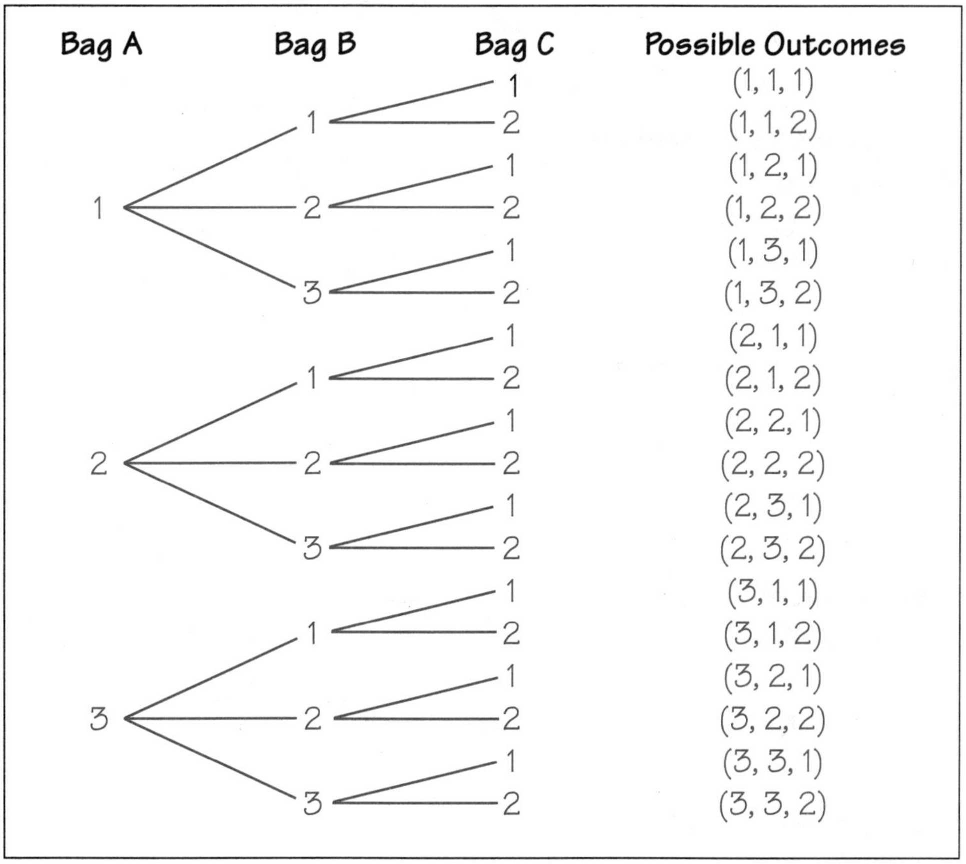

Use your tree diagram to answer these questions.

8. **How many outcomes are possible?** 18

9. **In how many outcomes are all three numbers the same?** 2

10. **In how many outcomes are there at least two 2s?** 6

TEST-TAKING PRACTICE

Choose the best answer for each problem. In the answer section at the bottom of this page, fill in the box of your choice.

Use this experiment for problems 1–5. Suppose you drew a letter from each box.

EAR	OR	ORE

1. **How many outcomes are possible?** D

   A 8   C 12
   B 9   D 18

2. **For how many outcomes will all of the letters drawn be the same?** J

   J 1   L 4
   K 2   M 5

3. **For how many outcomes are at least two of the letters *R*s?** C

   A 4   C 6
   B 5   D 7

4. **In how many outcomes is at least one letter an *O*?** M

   J 6   L 9
   K 8   M 12

5. **In how many outcomes is one letter an *A*?** A

   A 6   C 9
   B 8   D 12

Write About It

Explain how you would make a tree diagram to solve this problem.

6. **Suppose you toss three counters that are red on one side and blue on the other side. In how many possible outcomes will at least one counter show red?**

Possible Answer: List the possible outcomes for tossing one counter. Then draw branches to match each outcome with the possible outcomes for tossing another counter. Extend each of the branches to show the possible outcomes for tossing the third counter. Then list the possible outcomes.

1. A ☐ B ☐ C ☐ D ☒   4. J ☐ K ☐ L ☐ M ☒
2. J ☒ K ☐ L ☐ M ☐   5. A ☒ B ☐ C ☐ D ☐
3. A ☐ B ☐ C ☒ D ☐

Name ____________________ **Chapters 1–12**

Test-Taking Skill: Trying Out the Answer Choices

If you have trouble solving a problem or finding an answer, decide on the kind of answer you need. Then, try out the different answer choices. This method can help you find the correct answer.

Example

The stadium seats 74,000. For the game, about 52,000 tickets were sold. About what percent of the stadium's capacity was that?

A 22,000 seats **C** 70%
B 30% **D** 100%

Step 1: Decide on the kind of answer you need.

The answer will be a percent.

Step 2: Try each answer choice.

Choice	Think	Is this the answer?
A: 22,000 seats	This is the wrong kind of answer.	No, the question asks for a percent.
B: 30%	An estimate, $\frac{1}{3}$ of 75,000 = 25,000, gives too small a number.	No, 30% of 74,000 is about 25,000.
C: 70%	Multiply: 0.7 x 74,000 = 51,800	Yes, 70% of 74,000 is 51,800. That's about right.
D: 100%	This cannot be the answer.	No, not all the seats were filled.

Step 3: Choose the correct answer, and fill in the correct square in the answer section. C

1. A ☐ B ☐ C ☒ D ☐

TEST-TAKING PRACTICE

Choose the best answer for each problem. In the answer section at the bottom of this page, fill in the box of your choice.

1. Marta wants to leave a 20% tip at a restaurant. The bill is for $7.95. **How much should she leave?** B

A $0.80 C $3.20
B $1.60 D $7.95

2. In 1997, 70% of the music albums sold were CDs. Just 4 years earlier, CDs had 20% less of the market. **What percent of albums sold in 1993 were CDs?** K

J 20% L 60%
K 50% M 70%

3. Pele made the exact color of red he wanted by mixing 6 drops of Scarlet paint with 4 drops of Fire Orange. He has 12 jars of Scarlet. **How many jars of Fire Orange does he need to mix with the Scarlet to make the same shade?** C

A 4 jars C 8 jars
B 6 jars D 12 jars

4. Bernie spent 2 hours doing his homework. He spent $\frac{1}{3}$ of that time on his math homework. How long did it take him to do his math homework? M

J 6 minutes L 20 minutes
K 12 minutes M 40 minutes

5. Nancy has a recipe that calls for 2 cups of nuts for every 6 cups of dough. She wants to use 8 cups of nuts. **How much dough does she need?** C

A 8 cups C 24 cups
B 12 cups D 48 cups

6. Ralph needs new socks. Sockorama sells 3 pairs for $7.50. The Sox Box has a sale on 4 pairs for 20% off its regular price of $10.00. **Where will Ralph get the best buy on one dozen pairs of socks?** K

J Sockorama L $24.00
K The Sox Box M $30.00

1.	A ☐	B ☒	C ☐	D ☐	**4.**	J ☐	K ☐	L ☐	M ☒
2.	J ☐	K ☒	L ☐	M ☐	**5.**	A ☐	B ☐	C ☒	D ☐
3.	A ☐	B ☐	C ☒	D ☐	**6.**	J ☐	K ☒	L ☐	M ☐